The Writing on the Wall

Essays on Culture and Politics

The Writing on the Wall

Essays on Culture and Politics

Himani Bannerji

TSAR
Toronto
1993

The publishers acknowledge generous assistance
from the Ontario Arts Council and the Canada Council.

ISBN 0-920661-30-0

TSAR Publications
P.O. Box 6996, Station A
Toronto, M5W 1X7 Canada

Contents

Introduction *vii*

Nostalgia for the Future: The Poetry of Ernesto Cardenal 1

The Poetry of Dionne Brand 24

Andrei Tarkovsky: A Discourse on Desire and History 40

Evenings Out: Attending Political Theatre in West Bengal 48

Language and Liberation: A Study of Political Theatre in West Bengal 62

Representation and Class Politics in the Theatre of Utpal Dutt 73

Nation and Class in Communist Aesthetic and the Theatre of Utpal Dutt 93

One Woman, Two Women, Without Women: Gender Construction in Bengali Theatre 126

The Alienated Hero in the Novels of Sunil Gangyopadhyay 138

Introduction

To articulate the past historically does not mean to recognize it "the way it really was" (Ranke). It means to seize hold of a memory as it flashes up at a moment of danger. Historical materialism wishes to retain that image of the past which unexpectedly appears to man singled out by history at a moment of danger. The danger affects both the content of the tradition and its receivers. The same threat hangs over both: that of becoming a tool of the ruling classes.

WALTER BENJAMIN *Theses on the Philosophy of History*

It is 1993. I am sitting in a cafe, a grey drizzle falls endlessly. The awning of the shops on the other side of the street are flapping in a strong wind. A tree reaches out skeletal fingers to the sky, and under the bare tree, barely covered in a fraying blue parka, a young man darts out a raw pink hand at passersby.

"Spare any change? Anything will do."

I think of a phrase from T S Eliot, something about "the winter of our discontent."

In the newspaper, a photograph. A US marine's foot on the back of a black man lying on the ground. The man's head is up, he is looking into the camera. His eyes are bullets. UN/US peace-keeping in Somalia.

In the newspaper again, a twenty-two-year-old Serbian male, soldier, convicted for rape and murder of Muslim women in prison camps. One hundred and fifty men. Every three days. Each time a woman gang-raped and murdered. "I had to shoot each time, because I was the lowest in rank." Herak. *Globe & Mail,* February '93.

"Come on, face it, socialism failed us, failed itself. Face it, Marx is dead. Face it, socialism . . . " Overheard in a cafe.

"What has class to do with it? It is about culture. It is about subjectivities. It is about agencies." Also in a cafe. "You can't name it, except in each locality." Being. Impenetrable. No understanding possible, no speaking about, only for. From the heart of experience, eyes look out, tongues speak. Or do they? "The subaltern cannot speak." Do we hear? Can we? Reality - the resonance, the "om" of discourse. Such distances encoded in our differences. No one dreams of "a common language" any more? Each alone next to the other, within the boundaries of skin, sex, discourse, locality, group, identity, ethnicity, religion, culture . . . Where are we? What happened to our kit of maps, compass, the North Star? Hidden in clouds? A ship in the dark. What are those shapes which surround us?

1993. "NAFTA WE DON'T HAFTA." Writing on the wall. Canada. Population 25 million, approximately. About 150,000 or more unemployed in Ontario alone. "Can your labour force be as flexible as the economy?" Mines close. Industries move. Ravage of "free" trade zones in that other world, the third in the Lord's scheme. Development. Structural adjustment. Sustainable development. Not revolutions sustained, but development empowers. No one says class, no one says capital. No one says imperialism. As he said, "no one talks like that any more. Class is an obsolete category. Only you do." A young neo-nazi male, crew-cut, green fatigues, brown not blue eyes, holds up a placard. "Super-Race, Aryan." Gypsies, sixty thousand, are sent back to Rumania. Germany cannot absorb any more "foreigners." Fire in the barracks of refugees. Vigil in candlelight. Nights of black crystal. "Never again." But Japan is "our" enemy. The wicked Saddam, the Satan of the East. Dragons rise in South East Asia. Where is Europe's St George? He advances under the sign of the eagle, radiant in his nuclear glory. Our times. 1993. Now.

Then. The essays in this book were written then, over a long period of time, when many "posts" which fence our times were not erected yet. The war in Vietnam had unified progressive people in protest against US imperialism. In the streets of Toronto, Canada, in 1974, there was rejoicing when the Yankees went home. Now in musicals such as *Miss Saigon* we lament the tragedy of a young American G I going home, leaving behind a seventeen-year-old Vietnamese prostitute. She loved one of the men who came with erect penises and weapons. Susan Brownmiller, in *Against Our Will*, speaks of rape squads being maintained by the US army in Vietnam. All forgotten. Now are we sorry that the Americans lost in Vietnam?

The essays in this book are bound together with a common set of political assumptions and a coherent social analysis, which connects culture and politics in ways that show their formative integrity. The political assumptions are, simply speaking, unapologetically (the time for that had not yet arrived) Marxist-socialist. Whether speaking of theatre in West Bengal, poetry in Nicaragua, or celebrating a young Caribbean poet in Toronto, they speak of a possibility of people making their own history, even though not exactly as they please. If it were as they wanted, there would be no need to die, to fight for what is justly theirs - the earth that they till, the industries that they produce, a culture that they create, a living life that is theirs. No contras. No embargoes. No Renamos. No World Bank. No IMF. No US/UN refereeing the world's struggles. In the simple lyrics of a working-class singer, Arlene Mantle:

Everywhere the right is rising
People we are organizing
Smash the right, is our song
Because we know that the right is wrong.

Enough. Naive on my part? On the part of all those who fought against increasingly highly technological wars with their courage and took on hand combats with death squads, like "La Mano Blanca"? Sentimentality? Romanticism? The realists and pragmatists of 1993 tell me that. After all, we lost, didn't we? Socialism, national liberation movements in the Third World were brought to their knees, weren't they, in supervised elections by the US/UN combine? The Soviet Union disappearing into smoke like a genie from a bottle in children's stories. Proof of the pudding, as they say, is in the eating. But I ask them, was the pudding ever brought to the table? Who was the knave that stole the tarts that the Queen of Hearts baked? I remain very suspicious, not about naivete, or revolutionary romanticism, but about the pragmatism of our "postindustrial, postmodern, postsocialist, posthuman" world. What stubborn foolishness to pit revolutionary social construction against radical cultural deconstruction. But there you are. That's what kept me writing - pieces here and there, combining what people do, how they live, with what they say about themselves. Certainly about "culture" and about "discourse," but whose "culture"? "Discourse" of what? And to what end?

These to me are the most pressing questions involving actual producers of cultures and discourses whose experiences are deeply implicated in and constructive of the social relations, everyday practices and histories within which they live. The present day cultural theories seem to constantly steer us away from them, making reality derivatively related to discursivity, floating and proliferating cultures over the grimy rooftops of societies.

In my case, for whatever they are worth, these critical essays were attempts to make sense of culture's (for example theatre, literature, cinema) relationship to what I had grown up calling the realms of the political and the historical. Issues spinning out of colonialism, imperialism, class and gender, not as discretely existing objective categories, but as social and ideological moments of each other, riveted my attention, thrilled and puzzled me. I wrote these essays at different times, on different genres of art, or discursive formal practices - call these artifacts and formal manifestations or what you will - deeply conscious of the integrity of the social and the cultural. And I sought to make spatial connections as well, reworking the geography of our globe through historical and current imperialist relations of ruling and resistance. Coming from India, hearing of the "Third World" as a political entity, as that vast stretch on the globe where colonialism ravaged yesterday and imperialism seeks to overpower today, in Toronto I met it face to face. The abstraction of the political category broke into countless faces of reality - people, languages, music and reports of struggles were all around me. I was learning about Africa, Latin America, walking the streets in solidarity demonstrations. I who could barely tell when I came to Toronto in 1969 where Nicaragua was, was eventually able to recount Sandino's struggles, look up to Ernesto Cardenal, read Marquez's great novel about history, consciousness and revolution, experience the bitterness of Allende's murder in 1973, and many other remembered and forgotten events and experiences. My one hundred years of solitude were also over. Like the young Aureliano Buendia the Second, I too had entered history and time. Connections between then and now, here and there, the personal and the social, the political and the personal, were fast becoming clear to me. In the presence, eyes, voices and expressions of my fellow passengers in the subway, for example, I understood what colonialism and imperialism mean, and what a long chain it is that bound and binds us, and where these manacles are forged.

So, insisting on a relational and reflexive critique, these essays are not in the genre of a recent (through the 1980s upto now) tradition of radical cultural theorization. Namely, they are not a critique of colonial discourse. They belong to a less discursively dominated mode. They come from a simpler, more innocently Marxist tradition of commitment to class struggle and national liberation movements. Notions such as "ambivalence," used by critics such as Homi Bhabha, for example, however complex they may be in deconstructing colonial discursivities, have no place in these much humbler essays, which see colonialism and imperialism in the black and white of resistance and oppression. Taking sides, believing that things can change, fighting for it, an activist epistemology grounded in commitment, are what provide the entry points, ground and end of these excursions. Actualities and possibilities of culture for resistance and ruling are my preoccupation. Themes such as social formations, class struggle in the capitalist societies of the Third World (mindful of the colonial and imperialist constraints and contexts), elaborated both within and from the outside, become topics of exploration rather than the colonizer's construction of us as "others." Consequently, the cultural productions are generally read through a framework of a double contradiction, that of imperialist relations between the "Western," especially the Anglo-American, countries and the Third World, as well as class relations within these countries themselves and their political forms. To understand what I mean, one may look at the essays on political theatre in West Bengal, the revolutionary poetry of Ernesto Cardenal, or the novels of Sunil Gangopadhyay, a very popular novelist of the last few decades in Bengal. The last essay, for example, discusses/displays how it is that this novelist projects and legitimates an Indian variety of the capitalist ethic of possessive individualism, investing the resulting alienation of this competitive individual with the honour of anguish. But the class character of this "hero" or the novel can not be understood concretely if we overlook the fact that this current phase of the Bengali novel, which may be termed as its "americanization," offers us a very particular context and form for consumption. Whatever the cultural form, then, my interest has been to explore it in terms of aesthetic construction, politics and social formations of what has been variously called national, indigenous and substantive subjectivities and agencies. Instead of entering through the topic of the "colonial subject," which in any case is always a colonial object, I have begun from the other end, our/my own, from a "third" world that exists in its many dimensions outside of the colonizer's grasp - though not without reference to it. In these spaces, in other societies and histories, fully formed subjects exist, grow, struggle, make their mistakes, win their victories, without caring what the so-called West thinks of them or without asking its permission.

The essays in this book should thus be read both in terms of their specificities and their general theoretical implications. Those on IPTA and Utpal Dutt's communist theatre, though a particular exploration of Indian cultural activities, also deal with the general issue of unsettled relations between "nation" and "class," a malaise from which communist parties everywhere seem to suffer. "Evenings Out" displays an attempt at experientially exploring the social relations and theatrical forms of representation of class, showing how even with the best of intentions the middle-class left can or does usurp the cultural political spaces of the subaltern classes whom they advance as revolutionary agents. The essay on Cardenal celebrates the allegories and metaphors of a popular liberation movement, read through a biblical cosmology, problematizing in the end the relationship between liberation theology and Marxism. In the present crisis of communism, socialism and Marxism on a global scale, these particularities of political-cultural attempts need to be seriously re-examined.

The theme of representation of class brings me to speak of the issues of representation and identity on a different count. These topics are central to any discussion of culture, but seem to be understood differently in different historical moments. Though it is claimed both by the left and the right that identity and representation have surfaced as cultural-critical topics in a post-Marxist, postmodern era, the actuality is that they were always there. The classical/orthodox communist tradition struggled with the formal and content dimensions of representing classes and class struggle. As I point out in the essay on language and liberation in the Indian People's Theatre Association, the entire tradition of socialist realism (a child of Soviet communist art) offered an iconic, synthetic version of the contending classes. Who has not seen this pre-scribed wicked bourgeois/landlord of a Punch & Judy show, in an unto-the-death confrontation with the well-muscled morally pure proletarian hero? Whatever we think of the types of identities and forms of representation ascribed in these cultural texts, we have to admit that they are structured around these themes. Other than these textual attempts, there has been activist advancing of identities, political self-namings, no less "cultural" than those of being a "woman of colour," a "black man," a "black woman," "gay and lesbian," a "queer nation" and so on. To be a "Sandinista" then, or to be a "feminist," a "communist," and so on, are also identities; they too call for their representational modalities. The poetry of Ernesto Cardenal is a voice projecting one version of these political-social identities. What then is the difference between these identities put forward by various political cultural subjects and those currently advanced in the context of cultural representation?

Among several differences there are a few I wish to emphasize. The identities that were named as "the proletariat," for example, or even as "feminist," can be seen as coding both a political position and an aspiration or desire. They are, to put it simply, identities of "becoming," expressing a creative and political need on someone's part. They are not of the so-called community or culture we were born into. They are what we forge in a process of social and political becoming. One is not born, given the commonsense and social organization of the world's history of patriarchy, a feminist. One painfully, at great price and joy, becomes one. Similarly, the same is at work in becoming communist, and so on. These political subjectivities have a content dimension as well, specially defining what we are *not,* and stressing what we are becoming. The "identities" advanced in the current difference bid, when considered in terms of politics, history and desire, are generally those of "being." They are about who we *are,* born into, originally and fundamentally - the "truth" about us. They signal a journey which is going forward by going inward or to the past. They do not signal, *as such,* a moral/political position. That one is a "South Asian woman," for example, has no discernible political feature, but rather a homogenized, synthesized cultural physiognomy. Unlike the identities of becoming, which display a politics, a social analysis about power and exploitation, especially emphasizing patriarchy, capital or class, these identities of being gesture towards cultural content and cultural boundaries. While an "identity" of a communist is based on an undertaking to do class struggle, thereby gesturing towards a general relational social being which implicates others as well, and thus widens the points of identification, the identities of being cultural, of nationalism, can not particularly tolerate the inclusion of class. So, even our existence within a racist/imperialist capitalism, which in the first place "makes the differences," can not be directly apprehended from this cultural/originary naming process.

Identities of being, however, can veer towards a revolutionary position when they are historicized and politicized. Dionne Brand's poetry, for example, as my essay states, is a good example of such a complex reworking of a black woman's identity. Her poems do not lead to a cultural nationalism, but rather to an anti-imperialist revolution, because the identity which is forged by exploring the being of a black woman in history is consciously displayed through a set of social relations of oppression unfolding in a capitalism based on slavery in the historic societies of the Caribbean. The essay on Andrei Tarkovsky's cinema explores this same question of identity in terms of history, memory and desire. Much of his work shows a constant breaking of boundaries, from a named self to the openness of a forming one.

There is very little in this book about "gender, race and class," about local situations, with the exception of one essay on the presence or absence of women in Bengali theatre. Even this essay is more interesting for exploring the essentially gendered nature of class, than as a specific exploration of women's situation in colonial or modern Bengal. And in the same vein, the thematization of racism with regard to Brand's poetry is less about that issue per se, than for bridging the colonial and imperialist spaces. It is a conscious decision on my part to exclude the essays on these themes and focus mainly on Third World politics and culture. My intention is to insist on the relevance of locating general theoretical/political explorations in these "othered" countries which are stereotypically represented in terms of confusion, squalor and apathy. In the Western conventional wisdom, they are to be pitied and rescued, even as victims of the West perhaps, but it follows from this very logic of representation that it is by the same imperial centres that they are to be saved, led, modernized. The book then does perform an overall antiracist exercise in insisting on posing the problematic of culture and politics outside of Canada and in general terms. We can enter the cultural-political arena in different names; let us say, here we enter in the name of a popular revolution. One more time we can say class, we can say capital and imperialism. Our subjectivities, agencies and identities won't vanish into the rarefied air of abstraction and generalities. Look around, there may be somebody out there to identify with - a comrade.

These essays are very specific, limited to a certain political analysis, a certain period of time in history, yet reaching out to linger in the memory of my readers. They are a response to what surrounded me at the time, and an attempt to think through political cultures which attended the period of my own growth. They are a way of making my own political statements, much in the manner of graffitti on the walls of big cities. A whole range of political positions, images, testimonials to one's having been there, a witness to events of our time in history. The rise and fall of the Bolshevik revolution, for example - what is one to make of my essay on communist theatre in Calcutta now, in the present juncture? With Nicaragua, now under UNO, what does the poetry of Ernesto Cardenal mean, since the Sandinista project was strangled by a sustained US seige, disguised as contra offensives? With a spectacular rate of unemployment in Canada, with tightening refugee/immigration laws, neo-Nazi forces such as the Heritage Front actively organizing in schools, how does one read the poetry of Dionne Brand? I don't say that the material I have worked on and my questions have no relevance for the present time. In fact quite the contrary. History and questions asked in an earlier phase have much to teach us. As remarked by Walter Benjamin, the angel of history looks back while being propelled forward. The violent storm that drives the angel forward, in Benjamin's time and ours, has proved to be the growth convulsions of capital. We need to ask questions of what preceded us in cultural-political projects; we also need to celebrate what was achieved. Benjamin's angel of history looks back to memory. So this writing on the wall is a great deal of what is left to us. Our own, and those of others before us. Rubbed-out forms and letters leap out to us: tongues of fire licking a bus, a part of a hammer-and-sickle, the sickening aura of half a swastika, a meditation on violence against women, claims and promises, with the name faded, " . . . was here."

A brief note should also be added regarding the format of these essays. In these days of standardization, every text is to be the mirror image of the other, following the same formal conventions. This is not the case with this book. They were mostly written for cultural magazines which did not care for the conventions of academic papers. So footnoting often gave place to quotations, with citations of titles of works. In a few cases, such as the essays on Utpal Dutt or the Indian People's Theatre Association, the notes are in the body of the text with an appended list of references. My advice to the reader would be to read the content, enjoy and query the ideas, the mode of expression, and not get overly preoccupied with footnotes. What is needed is in the body of the text, that is where the conversation is centred.

I also wish to acknowledge a deep debt of solidarity, to my many comrades who have helped me to think, have helped in keeping my faith and sanity alive. I particularly wish to thank Michael Kuttner, who offered loving technical and moral assistance - that classic line fits here completely, without him these essays would not exist on paper, but merely as ideas in my head.

Nostalgia for the Future: The Poetry of Ernesto Cardenal

In October 1983, in a packed auditorium at the Ontario Institute for Studies in Education (Toronto), Ernesto Cardenal, poet, priest and Nicaragua's minister of culture in the Sandinista government, spoke about his country's desperate and courageous attempts to hold on to the revolution of 19 July 1979 and nurture it to its fullest development. Speaking of Nicaragua as a country beseiged by economic and military aggression of the United States, Cardenal also emphasized the country's role as an emblem of hope in the Latin American and Caribbean struggle against imperialism. "Are we exporting revolution?" he asked with a smile. "I don't know about that, but we are certainly exporting hope." Cardenal took pains to explain the Nicaraguan path to revolution: "In four years of revolution Nicaragua has experienced profound changes, material as well as spiritual. The Nicaraguan revolution is a new one, without models. It is an original Nicaraguan revolution."

What, we might ask, is the originality of Nicaragua's revolution? Cardenal outlined its main features for us. It characterized by a mixed economy, it is popular and humanistic. Speaking about humanism, he remarked that this was the "most generous revolution in history . . . the first without the death penalty." As Sandinista leader Tomaso Borge put it, "In Nicaragua what has been executed is the past." This humanism is complemented by an all-pervasive presence of Christian ethics:

> It is the first to be achieved with the mass participation of Christians. The reason is that the revolution was of the majority and that majority are Christians. It's not only that there are many priests in the government, but that there are many active lay people who hold government and cabinet posts. (*Christians in the Nicaraguan Revolution*)

The popular aspect of the revolution becomes evident when the massive participation of women as well as that of young people of both sexes is considered:

> Nicaragua's second largest city, Leon, was liberated by a twenty-three-year-old woman commander, as were other cities. Today's army and police are made up of Sandinistas, which is to say, of many young women members.

And as for young people, suffice it to say that "at one time the most wanted person by the guard was a twelve-year-old revolutionary. They found him one day and killed him." And finally Cardenal spoke about the collective nature of the leadership in Nicaragua.

Another aspect of Nicaragua's revolution, although not mentioned initially, began to be highlighted as the evening wore on. In the middle of the talk and questions about the political situation in Nicaragua some one introduced words like "culture" and "poetry." But Cardenal had not come to Canada this time in his capacity as a poet, and he declined to read or recite from any of his poems. He remarked good-humouredly that a poet must forget his old poems in order to write new ones. Instead he spoke about the importance of cultural work as a process of socialist reconstruction. When speaking of culture he extended the conventional use of this term to speak of a culture of political economy, a cultural dimension of health care and the people's militia, pointing out that every project of reconstruction includes a cultural wing, through which people problematize their needs and raise consciousness. New and old cultural forms, verbal and nonverbal, are used. While this was reminiscent of the theories and practices of the Brazilian educationist Paolo Freire, what was important and original about Cardenal's position was not that he expanded the use of a certain device, but that he actually created the possibility of rethinking a body of work, activities and values which we call culture.

Making a Cultural Revolution

With this definition of cultural work, Cardenal, like many other politically committed artists, shifts from a conventional way of thinking about creative work towards a new aesthetic. It is not only that art, or "culture," may be used to serve the people in understanding and expressing something, but also that it must reformulate itself in terms of social relations. Our conventional use of this term has been largely a topographical one; we use it to mark out a certain realm of activities, a certain aspect of our social geography. Culture in that sense is like a fence, a boundary, outside of which lie our noncultural activities, whatever they may be. But how do we know how to classify some activities as cultural and others as not? The conventional practice has gone to various formal traditions, types of media and mediations, in establishing what qualifies a culture and what does not. That is, we have a cultural product index. We don't see it so much as an activity in the context of ongoing social relations but as an end product of a certain type, constructed within certain "genres" or traditions.

In Cardenal's terms, however, it is possible to see culture not only as a previously coded body of products but also as a set of expressive formalizing activities in the context of an ongoing set of social relations. Any change in the social relations can and indeed must bring about major changes in our formalizing expressive activities - in their location, use and form. Perhaps then it is possible to say about culture what once Marx said about capital: that it is not a thing but a set of social relations concretized within history and formal traditions. So when new social relations evolve, in the process of creating revolution or in the postrevolutionary era, they lead to a redifinition of culture both as a category and as activity. This way of seeing of course provides an activist role for a population of producers of their own culture rather than the passive one of consumers of "art" turned out by the socially disengaged artist. Cardenal himself has written about this in many of his poems, particularly in the context of language and culture, in the collection *Zero Hour and Other Documentary Poems*:

> Revolutionary art without artistic value . . .
> And artistic art without revolutionary value? It seems to me
> that great bards of the 20th century are in Publicity
> those Keatses and Shelleys singing the Colgate smile
> Cosmic Coca-Cola, the pause that refreshes
> . . . .
> language, also polluted.
> It appears that he (Johnson) never understood
> that words also have a real meaning
> besides serving for propaganda
> *Time* said that he does understand it and he lies just the same.
> And the defoliation of Vietnam
> is a Resource Control Program
> it's also a defoliation of language.
> And language avenges itself refusing to communicate.
> Plunder: investments.
> There are also crimes of the CIA in the realm of semantics.
> Here in Nicaragua, as you have said:
> the language of the government and private enterprise

against the language of the Nicaraguan people.
("Epistle to Jose Coronel Urtecho")

This view of language and art, that is of culture, suggests the need for a new aesthetic. A revolutionary struggle is also a cultural one; that is, it is a struggle for the reclamation of our everyday lives, for our right to express and communicate in our own way. And this struggle which is cultural-political is also personal because it involves making a choice, deciding what kind of social relations one wishes to live with, and this means knowing which side one is on. It is at this level that Ernesto Cardenal's poetry addresses its readers, as a personal message outlining the task of a personal political choice - particularly about Nicaragua.

In fact, Cardenal's poems are a lot like letters to the individual reader. They are an invitation for participation, for making a choice, and they demand a clear yes or no about their content. There is no standing by in an objectivist pose and watching in an act of abstract contemplation. Of course the reader may delay for a while, wander about with the book in a handbag, defer coming to any conclusions because that involves so many confusions, doubts, indecisions - but position oneself one must, or the process of reading this poetry will not be concluded. Cardenal is not a liberal relativist saying, "This is only my version of Nicaragua; you may have one too. Both are equally tenable, or the truth lies in between." His vision is totally integrated with the revolutionary efforts of the Sandinistas, and he speaks with the absolute moral imperative of the revolutionary, and this absolutism is compounded by the morality of "liberation theology." If this version of history and social change is not to any reader's liking, if that reader also rejects this absolute moral imperative, then Cardenal is not his or her poet. And today in North America and elsewhere the world is divided between people who say yes to this political stand of Ernesto Cardenal and those who do not.

Cardenal's version of the world in which we live - in which Nicaragua lived - is simply the world of industrial capitalism in its imperialist phase; it is not meant for the advancement of people but profit. A world of "Texaco, Standard Oil . . . the monopolies," a world evolved from a long history of class societies, of "private property and the accumulation of capital."

Later on better than raising sheep was stealing sheep.
War could be an industry.
To guard the wheat as important as sowing it.
War could be productive.

And after domesticating animals man invented a way
to domesticate man.
Not killing the enemy: making him work.
Slavery was the basis of industry and the accumulation of capital . . .
The division of classes a product of progress? Yes
but it did not accelerate, it retards future progress.
Progress in neolithic times was in the production processes
and it was made by the producers
but now these - the inventors - become
the lower class.

A world of beauty, of "Moon pottery / (white laquer and fine-lined motifs). Charming / red jaguars with a white background, incense pots" had fallen prey to imperialist enterprises. On top of the world of freshness and beauty lay:

bits of Coca-Cola bottles and Goodyear tires and chamber pots.
Acahualinca begins there, the houses of cardboard and cans
where the sewers empty . . .
Streets that smell of jails,
that characteristic jail smell
of shit and rancid urine
houses of cement bags gasoline cans rubble old rags.
The sewers end there.
. . . .
There the children with wary little eyes
the children weak sickly enormous beetles
their bellies swollen and their legs thin as toothpicks . . .
. . . .
Old women crouched over the guts that the slaughterhouse throws out
scaring off the buzzards.
The pig and the pot-bellied kid in the same puddle.
. . . .
I saw a papaya tree in a street like a miracle in that horror.
("Oracle over Managua")

This is clearly a degraded and inverted world. The humans have been denied all conditions of being human. "Man's greatest crime is to prevent men from being men." And to be set back on its feet, to be the right way up it must be turned upside down, a complete reversal. Hence revolution. Cardenal's poetry is full of insurrectionary, resurrectionary (which for him is also revolutionary) signs. Revolution is to be seen as a communion at the end of a long chapter of exploitation.

kupia-kumi = "one-single-heart"
One-single-heart: the military and money look like that
today (but those two have no heart). No: the sole true kumi
is Love, namely the union of the people to achieve
the Revolution. Only Love is truly single-heart.
("Nicaraguan Canto")

And so for Cardenal. Revolution is inscribed as the last stage in the book of nature, in the evolutionary process; a denial of the revolution is the denial of God's will as expressed through nature.

I said the iguanas lay their eggs . . . It is the process. They
(or else the frogs) in the silence of the carboniferous age
made the first sound
sang the first love song here on earth
sang the first love song here beneath the moon
it is the process.
The process started with the stars.
New relations of production: that too
is part of production: that too
is part of the process. Oppression. After oppression, liberation.
The Revolution started in the stars, millions
of light years away.
("Nicaraguan Canto")

These lines are not simply a matter of metaphors, poetic licence; Cardenal means what he says. He is rather a literal writer and for him the Bible, nature and the revolutionary process are inextricably intertwined, in that together they illuminate the truth. The belief that holds him in the position of the minister of culture in the face of Vatican opposition and away from a life of contemplation is also articulated in the lines that follow. They are not merely "poetic" moments or biblical metaphors, but a guide to conduct.

Because at times a man is born in a land
and he *is* that land.
And the land in which that man is buried

is that man.
And the men who afterward are born in that land
are that man.
And Adolfo Baez Bone was that man.
("Nicaraguan Canto")

The Land, the Man

Ernesto Cardenal was born into a well-to-do family in Granada, Nicaragua, in 1925. He studied at the University of Mexico (1943-47) and Columbia University in New York (1947-49). During 1957-59 he was a novice at the Trappist monastery in Gethsemany, Kentucky, where poet and priest Thomas Merton was his spiritual director. Cardenal's ill-health, among other reasons, prevented him from taking the vow and he studied instead for the priesthood during 1959-65. In 1965 he returned to Nicaragua and established a church and a commune which he named Nuestra Senora de Solentiname. This place is an archipelago of thirty-eight islands on Lake Nicaragua, with a population of one thousand campesinos (peasants) and fishermen. In 1970 he went to Cuba to be a judge for a poetry competition organized by Casa de las Americas. In 1977 the Somoza dictatorship ordered the destruction of the commune and Cardenal fled to Costa Rica. Thereafter he became the roving ambassador for the liberation movement (FSLN) which in 1979 toppled the Somoza dictatorship. Cardenal was chosen to be the minister of culture in the new government.

A poet and writer for a long time, Cardenal is relativeley unknown to English readers. His books of poems which have received some attention in the English-speaking world are *Apocalypse and Other Poems* (English translation 1977) and *Zero Hour and Other Documentary Poems* (English translation 1981). Another work, *In Cuba* (English translation 1974), is an account of socialist reconstruction in Cuba and an assessment of Christianity's methods, goals and morality in relation to those of communism. The trip to Cuba convinced Cardenal of the compatibility of the two. *Homage to the American Indian* (English translation 1973) is virtually unknown among English readers and difficult to come by. There are also two other volumes, which consider the relationship of Christianity to revolutionary activities, and specifically ponder the question of armed struggle, namely, *The Sanctity of Revolution* (1976) and *The Gospel in Solentiname*. There is also a small illustrated book, published after the revolution, about Solentiname and Cardenal's own involvement there, called *Nostalgia del Futuro*.

These are the bare facts of Ernesto Cardenal'slife, and they have to be supplemented by other facts, contextualized in relation to the Nicaraguan reality. We must move out of individual biography to the history of the country, of the region and the relations of the US to Central America. Questions as to Cardenal's involvements before he became a priest, why he set up the commune of Solentiname, why it was destroyed, why he went to Cuba, how he can be part of a political group that espouses armed struggle, or a member of the state, far away from his priestly duties - these questions can only be answered by introducing the historical element into his personal life. Cardenal himself is acutely aware of being rooted in the Nicaraguan reality. In the "Nicaraguan Canto" comparing his poetry to the local birds' song, he expresses a complete identification with his country.

> I'd like to watch the lumberjacks at work.
> To talk to turtle-catchers on the cays.
> This is the land I sing. My poetry belongs here,
> like the trumpeting zanate, or the wine-producing palm.
> I feel a longing for those eastern swamps.

His poetry is an epic verse rendition of Nicarguan history and struggles, and it is to this history that we must now turn.

The history of Nicaragua has been one of a continuous battle against the local tyrants set up and propped up by US military power and the ubiquitous presence of the US multinationals or its adventurist gangsters, such as William Walker, earlier in this century. The attitudes and activities of the gangsters were actually not very different from those of the businessmen and the government interventions that were to follow, for example Cornelius Vanderbilt, the American railroad magnate who built an extensive empire in Central America, later companies such as the United Fruit Company, and even the White House itself. Always with the so-called business came the army. All talk by modern political theorists of the major capitalist countries about the "relative autonomy" of the state breaks down in the face of the imperialist ventures of their countries. The business and the state always go hand in hand. As Cardenal puts it,

> To invest capital in Nicaragua and then to protect
> US investments was the State Department's job.

And

> the marines landed to "reestablish order"
> and they stayed in Nicaragua for 13 years. Control

over railroads customs banks was not enough.
Nicaragua sold her territory as well . . .
("Nicaraguan Canto")

The Monroe Doctrine of 1823, which, as George Black points out in his book *Triumph of the People: The Sandinista Revolution in Nicaragua,* "claimed the Americas as an exclusive target for US expansionism in exchange for nonintervention in the colonial affairs of the European powers," is still in operation today. Whenever there is any attempt to move out of the US economic and military stranglehold, local and US repression descends. One such attempt led to the emergence of the liberation fighter Augusto Cesar Sandino in 1927, when "the US marines duly disembarked at Corinto in January. This time the force was a large one: 215 officers commanding 865 marines and 3900 soldiers, accompanied by arms supplies . . ." Sandino, whose memory lives in the revolution of Nicaragua today, was a thirty-one-year-old worker who had returned to the country after years of working for the US companies. In his account of the development of the Nicaraguan revolution, George Black outlines the nature of the resistance put up by Sandino and his guerillas from the mountains of Segovia:

> His experience as a worker was vital to the formation of his anti-imperialist and to an extent class consciousness. As a warehouseman in Montecristo sugar mill in Honduras owned by the Honduras Sugar and Distilling Company; as a banana plantation worker for the United Fruit Company in Guatemala; as an oilfield worker for the South Pennsylvania Oil Company and Huasteca Petroleum Company, he had learned his lessons in politics. It had given him a firsthand knowledge of the reality of American imperialism in Central America. Under Sandino's leadership, the war against US intervention was Nicaragua's first organized questioning of bourgeois and imperialist power structures, and gave shape for the first time to a long - if sporadic - tradition of spontaneous popular revolt.

For this resistance Sandino was murdered by Anastasio Somoza, the head of the National Guard, created by the US in 1934, and of course with the active support of the White House. Before he had him killed in an ambush, Somoza invited Sandino to Managua for peace talks and embraced him publicly.

How much of these events influenced Ernesto Cardenal? People make their own history, but they don't do it just as they please. The world into which we are born, its politics, history and culture, provides us with the stage on which we act, parts that we have to reconstruct for ourselves. Not even the strongest individual consciousness is solely self-determined and immune to history. The Nicaragua into which Cardenal was born echoed with the struggle and the betrayal of Sandino. For almost half a century thereafter Cardenal and Nicaragua lived through the dual realities of repression and resistance. His life coincides with the founding of the Somoza dynasty and goes beyond. Changing neither their master nor their economic and political practices, the Somozas continued to grow from 1934 until by the 1970s the state of Nicaragua had become the private estate of the family. To this the people offered their persistent resistance, so during his student days Cardenal, like other young people of the country, found himself joining in the resistance attempts, which culminated again in an armed struggle. People from all walks of life found themselves next to each other in this process. Cardenal's poetry is a tribute to such people, every line filled with a direct knowledge of their sacrifice, their torture and death.

> That same night a boy stripped to his shorts.
> Like one of those frightened puppies.
> "Drink it up," said Colonel Somoza Debayl to me. "Isn't it your own blood? It won't hurt you."
> I began to confess lies my voice faltering, the stenographers
> getting it down on paper with their swift pencils . . .
> Between one torture and the next he'd see a movie.
> ("Oracle Over Managua")

Countdown to the Revolution

In the poem "Zero Hour," written before Cardenal went to the Trappist monastery, we find the history of Nicaragua paralleled by Cardenal's own development; it is the countdown to the revolutionary moment. The poem is in four sections. The first section is an overview of Central America as a whole, narrowing down to Nicaragua.

> Tropical nights in Central America,
> with moonlit lagoons and volcanoes
> and lights from the presidential palaces,
> barracks and sad curfew warnings . . .
>
> And Managua the target of machine guns

from the chocolate cookie palace
and steel helmets patrolling the streets

Watchman! What hour is it of the night?

In the next section the particularity of Nicaragua is further specified, a country rendered to a carrion by the Somozas and their US allies, with the multinationals crawling in it like so many maggots, and terrible man-made famines stalking the land.

The banana is left to rot on the plantations,
or to rot in the cars along the railroad tracks
or it's cut overripe so it can be rejected
when it reaches the wharf to be thrown into the sea;
the bunches of banana declared bruised or too skinny,
or whithered, or green, or overripe, or diseased:
so there'll be no cheap bananas,
or so as to buy bananas cheap.

Having outlined the different stages and causes of oppression the poem introduces the theme of resistance. Augusto Cesar Sandino becomes the embodiment of Nicaragua's struggle against foreign and local dictatorships. Cardenal takes historical details of this struggle and its betrayal, and projects them until there is a fusion between the past resistance and that of the FSLN leading to a victory in 1979. It was also in these northern mountains, Sandino's Segovias, that the Sandinistas regrouped themselves for the final onslaught against the Somoza regime. There, beckoned by the light of revolution, which is also the light of Sandino,

What is that light way off there? Is it a star?
It is Sandino's light shining in the black mountains.
The old and the new Sandinistas fuse into one.
There they are, he and his men, beside the red bonfire
with rifles slung and wrapped in their blankets,
smoking or singing sad songs from the North,
the men motionless and their shadows in motion.

The following section about the failed uprising of 1954 moves closer to Cardenal's personal experience. It is about his friend Adolfo Baez Bone's death, but also about himself and all the others who fought. Sandino's death is repeated but this time not with a simple act of treachery, but through tanks and planes that raze the house that hid Bone and his companions.

> But April in Nicaragua is the month of death.
> They killed them in April.
> I was with them in the April rebellion
> and I learned to handle a Rising machine gun.
> And Adolfo Baez Bone was my friend:
> They hunted him with airplanes, with trucks,
> with floodlights, with tear-gas bombs,
> with radios, with dogs, with police;
> and I remembered the red clouds over the Presidential Mansion
> like blood-red swabs of cotton.

In "Nicaraguan Canto" and "Oracle Over Managua," Cardenal writes of these deaths again and again - the deaths of the poets Lionel Rugama, Ruben Dario, and all others who were part of the struggle - "Selim Shible, Silvio, Casimiro, Julio, they had fallen." And "Glory isn't what the history books teach: / it's a flock of buzzards in a field and a great stink." But the theme of the undying freedom fighter who rises up or returns because he died for his people, a common myth of many agrarian struggles, is also present in Cardenal's poetry. It keeps alive the hope, the continuity of the people's struggle. "The underground radio kept saying he was alive. / The people didn't believe he had died. / (And he hasn't died.)"

It was at this time (around 1954) that Cardenal seems to have turned to the church. When he went to the Trappist monastery at Gethsemane he couldn't have been very optimistic about anything, let alone about a successful armed uprising against the organized US-backed brutality of the Somoza regime. In this state, suffering from excruciating headaches, Cardenal was particularly fortunate in his spiritual director. It is Thomas Merton who gave him his new direction. In an interview with Margaret Randall, Cardenal gives us a brief history of the foundation of his contemplative activist community, Solentiname.

> It was Thomas Merton who gave me the idea. He had been a monk for twenty years and had written a great deal about that life but had been unhappy with monastic life . . . And after twenty years Merton was wanting out . . . He knew it was a medieval, anachronistic lifestyle. Ridiculous. So he wanted to found a different kind of contemplative

> community outside the US. Merton was an enemy of the US, of Yankee civilization and everything it represented. He hated the bourgeois mentality most monks had . . . He told me I was in my monastic honeymoon and that within a few years I too would find the life arid.
> (*Christians in the Nicaraguan Revolution*)

So Cardenal returned to his country and slowly developed the community of Our Lady of Solentiname. It was a long process of involvement in the life of the local people, becoming a part of their everyday life, not only as the priest in residence, but as a teacher, a friend. Much went on in this little community. The gospels were read, interpreted, poetry written, paintings done, and all the while the situation in Nicaragua examined, understood, actions considered in the light of new interpretations of the Bible in a communitarian context. Cardenal had once more turned to the struggle for the liberation of Nicaragua. Abstract contemplation, far from the world of pain and misery, was not to be his path. He engaged in what could be called "praxis" and combined the understanding of history with struggle for change. The people of this community had come to the same conclusions as he had. One of the older members of the community, Olivia, had this to say to Margaret Randall when questioned on how she felt about revolutionary militancy:

> Each day we would learn new things, and I tell you that this is the sort of thing where you couldn't take it in and just live in peace. You begin to feel more committed, more concerned about others. If, living the life we led, we were concerned about all our neighbours, now we had concern for everything in the country. And afterwards, for everything not only in the country but also in Central America. And for what was happening in the world. (*Christians in the Nicaraguan Revolution*)

There was an active contact with the FSLN, and many of the young people of the community became guerillas and joined the liberation movement. This brought down tremendous repression, and finally in 1977 Solentiname was destroyed by the National Guard. The physical destruction of the community could not break the spirit of the people however. Though Cardenal fled to Costa Rica, the members of the community who survived continued to fight along FSLN lines. Cardenal himself became a spokesman for the liberation movement and represented it at UN meetings and in various countries. On July 18 1979 he clandestinely flew back into the country. The next day Nicaragua was reborn from the ashes and debris of the past. In the poem

"Light" in *Zero Hour,* this moment of possibility finds its expression.

> It's the most dangerous moment, enemy aircraft
> may be waiting for us over the airport.
> And the airport lights at last.
> We've landed. From out of the dark come olive-green comrades
> to greet us with hugs.
> We feel their warm bodies, that also come from the sun,
> that are also light.
> This revolution is fighting the darkness.
> It was daybreak on July 18th. And the beginning
> of all that was about to come.

Christian Communism

The Nicaraguan revolution, said Cardenal, was a unique revolution. This would appear to be the case if in particular one were to consider the nature of its political mobilization. It is not so much a classically Marxist as a populist revolution. It realizes the dreams of both Christians and communists, one could even say of Christians as communists. How, the world has been asking, is that possible? After all, Christianity has been very ready to be of service to colonialism, imperialism and local exploitation. The cultural and ideological subjugation of the peoples of the Third World in the name of God, Christ and the church has been well recorded and much discussed. The Andean Indians who were declared to have no soul, and therefore to be of no consequence as human beings, were eliminated with the church's approval and help. The Africans who exchanged their land for the Bible, as the saying goes, lost more than their worldly possessions in the process. It is perhaps more than a piece of trivia that the first slave ship was called *Jesus*. (The examples of dissident Jesuits and priests do more than anything else to prove the exceptional nature of their commitment, rather than Christianity's positive contribution to the people's cause. The unpopularity of such clerics with the Vatican is also well recorded.)

The struggles of the poor during the last few centuries have not been able to sway the Catholic church or Christianity in general to act for them in any significant way. If there was once a contradiction between the church and growing capitalism (which appears upon close inspection to be a conflict of interest - feudalism fighting capitalism) there is certainly no vestige of that now. Once the church, though itself the biggest European landlord in the middle ages, forbade usury; now the Vatican has its own bank. Cardenal mentions this bank in "Zero Hour": "The Bank of the Holy Spirit has been closed. / A kind of automatic fruition, as if / money laboured."

By and large, as far as poor people are concerned, the church has operated on the dictum of "To him that hath it shall be given, but from him who hath not it shall be taken away." But it seems that time and time again the misery of the people and their social discontent catch up with their religious beliefs, and with or without sanction from the church institutions and ecclesiastical bodies, they proceed to put up their version of what God meant against the version of those in power. They speak in the language of religion because that is the clearest ideology that they have. And here we might mention from Marx the expressive aspect of religious ideology - not just the pacificatory one since so far we have only heard of a truncated quotation from Marx on religion as the opiate of the masses. The fuller version of what Marx actually said widens the social implications of religious expressions:

> Religious distress is at the same time the expression of real distress and also the protest against real distress. Religion is the sigh of the oppressed creature, the heart of a heartless world, just as it is the spirit of the spiritless condition. It is the opium of the people.

By the 1960s a popular and militant version of Christianity seemed to be emerging in Latin America. There was of course the impact of the Columbian priest Camillo Torres, excommunicated and killed, whose Christianity prompted him to pick up a gun to fight the exploitation of the rural poor in Columbia. And also there was a general disgust at the traditional church for its hand-in-glove complicity with the dictators. As Cardenal puts it,

> the church goes to bed with anyone at all . . .
> Monsignor Borgia all in red tassels and phylacteries
> presiding over the Bishop's conference
> "And that prick from Nazareth, what's he saying"
> . . . the apostasy of the Nicaraguan church . . .
>
> Fernando said: don't fuck around.
> Tinita Salazar doesn't earn ten pesos a week.
> Pijulito died because the hospital wouldn't let him in.
> And then they talk to me about God. Don't be ridiculous!
> ("Zero Hour")

Clearly if religion were going to mean anything for the people it had to be different from what the monsignors of this world had preached as the word of God. It would have to be a church that would not excommunicate the Camillo Torreses of Latin America. And a possibility arose from within the church itself for some reinterpretation to occur.

> The second Vatican Council called by Pope John XXIII in 1962 prescribed a gospel-oriented content for Christianity and a more socially conscious doctrine than that of previous papal encyclicals. A general ecumenical opening-up allowed for dialogue with other denominations and non-Christians. Lay people were given responsibility in the pastoral work of the church. Liturgical reforms included the introduction of language, songs and instruments native to different cultures and an end to masses in which priests kept their back to the people.
>
> (*Christians in the Nicaraguan Revolution*)

The Latin American Bishop's Conference in Medillin, Columbia, in 1968, concretized the radical implications of this new papal encyclical. "Liberation theology" began to be theorized and acted upon. The Catholic Church in Latin America had entered a new era. The long existing demand for equality of all people and social justice was now firmly anchored in the idea of a just God who punished the wicked and legitimized popular militancy against all forms of oppression. The life of Christ was read more directly, from the vantage point of the oppressed rather than mediated through the "institution." In fact the story of Christ became the story of the poor people themselves. Christ was seen as a poor revolutionary who sought justice for the poor and died on the cross of the ruling class. There was sought a return to the early pre-Constantine nonimperial days of the religion, to the days of the catacombs. Christianity was again to be a religion created by and for the poor, not that which was later adopted and radically adapted by the ruling class. There was an identification of the Christian in the catacombs with the guerilla going underground to avoid Somoza's National Guard. "With no alternative to death / You went underground / or as you said entered the catacombs." The mystical tradition reread thus could have profoundly political and incendiary possibilities. What actions should follow from lines such as these:

> The solution is simple: to give to others in brotherhood.
> Capitalism impedes communion.
> . . . .

Saint Ambrose thundered in his Milan cathedral, on the threshold
of feudalism . . .
THE EARTH BELONGS TO EVERYBODY, NOT THE RICH
and Saint John Chrysostom in Byzantium with his Biblical Marxism
"the community of goods is more faithful to nature."
("Zero Hour")

Both the priests and the lay Catholic community were aware of the radical and novel nature of this interpretation, but neither group considered it as heretical. In fact the traditional church's record of repression and class service had earned it the name of "church of hierarchy." Not only was Christianity reconcilable with militant class struggle, it also actually offered the imperative of militancy out of its own nature.

This particular way of reading Christianity provided the majority of the people with a world view, a language, a systematic organization of symbols and signs, a basis for the construction of the struggle. There was no need to learn a completely new way of conceptualizing and expressing; they could begin from where they were, transforming the world they inhabited. Part of the real social transformation was that very transformation of Christianity itself. It was both a tool for change and the tool forged in the struggle. God was called to be on the side of the poor, and it was felt that he was.

Visionaries and Revolutionaries

Such a large-scale reinterpretation of the Bible and formulation of social movements in terms of religious ideology is relatively new in the Catholic tradition. But Christianity had already served this purpose in the Protestant tradition. The peasants' war in Germany was fought in the name of Martin Luther, though he wanted no part in it, and the civil war in England, also called the "puritan revolution," activated large-scale religio-political movements. In the English case in particular, during the war and even through the period of restoration and the eighteenth century, religious ideas of different types served as the common people's ideology of social struggle.

Radical activist Christian sects such as Levellers, Diggers, Ranters, Shakers, Quakers and Muggletonians have mostly disappeared, leaving behind a luminous history of visions of social change. The influence of John Muggleton and other poor people's mystics - such as shoemaker Jacob Boehm - on William Blake's revolutionary poetry has been discussed at length by writers such as E P Thompson. John Bunyan's *Pilgrim's Progress* is another vision that has found its way into English literature.

The work of Cohn, *The Pursuit of the Millenium*, and that of Christopher

Hill, *The World Turned Upside Down,* document many of these revolutionary religious movements. Religion was such an integral force in the demand for social change that Christopher Hill made the remark that "Indeed it is perhaps misleading to differentiate too sharply between politics, religion and general skepticism." What he says of the seventeenth and eighteenth centuries is equally applicable to the popular revolutionary ideology of Central America.

Of course this reinterpretation was not a scholarly exercise, a textual debate on the Bible, but rather a way of exploring and realizing the ethical imperatives of a certain type of Christianity. People acted on the belief that it was "easier for a camel to pass through the eye of a needle than for the rich man to enter the kingdom of heaven." They also acted on the promise that "the meek shall inherit the earth," and made distinct attempts to attain the reward here and now. The kingdom of heaven would at least find its earthly expression in a new social order brought about by the militancy of the poor. It is illuminating to read in this context what the seventeenth-century Christian activist Gerald Winstanley said to the people of London:

> Freedom is the man that will turn the world upside down,
> therefore no wonder he hath enemies . . . True freedom lies in the
> community, in spirit and community in the earthly treasury, and
> this is Christ the true man-child spread abroad in the creation,
> restoring all things unto himself.
>
> (G Winstanley, *A Watch-Word to the City of London,* 1649)

The social project of the common people of Europe in the seventeenth and eighteenth centuries was not very dissimilar to that of the common people of Nicaragua in the 1970s. An echo of Winstanley's sentiment can be heard in the words of Olivia, a poor woman living in the community of Solentiname, whom I quoted earlier:

> Revolution and religion go together; they are two equal things, never unequal. That is why I say that revolutionaries can be Christian. There is no contradiction. I have heard some people say that a revolutionary can't be a Christian. In truth, is a revolutionary not a real Christian? If a revolutionary does not mention God perhaps it is because he or she doesn't want to. In fact he or she is more Christian than many who say they are . . . And any person who says they're very religious but they don't like the revolution must not understand Jesus.
>
> (*Christians in the Nicaraguan Revolution*)

But then again, this is not the seventeenth century and there are distinct aspects to the Nicaraguan religio-political ideology which are features of a post-Marxian era, filled with global anti-imperialistic struggles. Liberation theology, therefore, not only speaks of the rich and the poor, the just and the unjust, but also about relations between classes, and socio-economic systems of exploitation and foreign domination called capitalism and imperialism. It is in this that they can supercede the older millenarian movements, build a movement oriented to class struggle, make alliances with non-Christians and Marxists and participate in the revolutionary armed struggles and the Sandinista government. Neither in the lay Catholic population nor in its priests - such as Ernesto Cardenal, Fernando Cardenal, Miguel de Scoto, Uriel Molina and others - do we see any doubt about the values embodied in the Nicaraguan revolution.

Cardenal's visit to Cuba, recorded in his book *In Cuba,* was one of a series of assessments made by Catholics, particularly priests, of the goals of a socialist revolution in the light of Christianity. Cardenal, for instance, found that communists or socialists or Christians could make close alliances and aimed for the same type of social justice. He feels strongly that the ethical imperatives of communism and Christianity, based on basic human needs and against different types of alienation, overlap. Going by the doctrines and practices of liberation theology, one could say that a new brand of militancy has evolved in Central America, a militancy of "communist Christianity," and I emphasize the word "communist" since "community" and "communion" are at the root of this word.

The Poetics of Documentation

This "communist Christianity" constitutes not only the politics of Ernesto Cardenal, but his poetics as well. The documentary quality of his poetry combines with a contemplative tone like that of Thomas Merton in an epic form. These formal devices are as essential to Cardenal as documentary film or news formats are to other "reporters" and documentarians. In Cardenal's case, as a partisan to the revolution, he must explain the revolution to us, show the justice of his cause and demand that we take sides too. For this he needs a type of realism in his poetry, a realism which is not just disjointed bits of the social surface, but is more in the nature of a set of transparencies showing what is going on underneath and around them - in fact, the social relations, the contexts that produce and texture the surface. Here the "natural" is relieved of its work of being a substitute for life. Events, bits of history, details of landscape and businesses, are all slides inserted into an "epic" version of history which provides a systematic view of exploitation and resistance.

Cardenal's poetry, then, records what exists, bears witness to what happened and is happening, but at the same time it captures the transformative forces. He must be "documentary" and "revelatory" at the same time. The technical or formal aspects of his poetry combine with the Bible and Marx's *Capital* or *The Communist Manifesto,* not in a bid for eclecticism, but in an attempt at creating a new epistemology, a new way of knowing reality. The vast sweep of Cardenal's historic vision from the pre-Columbian days to now is also set within the Biblical myth of the fall, of "Paradise lost" through the conquest and regained through the revolution.

Because Cardenal is a Christian communist he can see the world as a set of signs from which a believer can read the will of God. This way of looking at the natural and social world presupposes of course a knowledge of, a commitment to, the Christian code, which confers significance to the world of appearances and events.

The elements of Cardenal's poetry include: descriptions, reports, allusions and certain types of juxtapositions where manmade horror, inflicted by imperialism, is juxtaposed with the beauty of nature. In fact, throughout his poetry the beauty of nature serves as a source of healing, a reminder of the possibility of regeneration. In poem after poem filled with stories of moral and economic bankruptcy, hunger and exploitation, death and torture of those who protest, there are also moments reflecting the serenity and innocence of Nicaragua's nature and her humble people. The early morning following Sandino's murder is an instance of this:

> It's the hour when the corn-mush star of Chontales
> gets the little Indian girls up to make corn mush,
> and out come the chicle-seller, the wood-seller, and the root-seller
> with the banana groves still silvered by the moon
>
> . . . .
>
> The ranch hands begin to herd their cows
>
> . . . .
>
> the boatmen hoist the sails of their boats;
>
> . . . .
>
> And the Tuca squaws keep coming down the Hidden River
> with the ducks going quack-quack-quack, and the echoes,
> the echoes, while the tugboat goes with the Tuca squaws
> slithering over the green-glass river
> toward the Atlantic . . .   ("Zero Hour")

This beauty of the natural world, set in contrast to Sandino's death, does not indicate nature's indifference to the goings-on in society, but rather resonates with the beauty of the "newly-created" earth! The beauty remains and the revolution's project is not only to reclaim the earth, but also to recreate a redemptive social order eliminating the contrast between the innocent beauty of nature and the socio-political world. "With all things held in common / as they were before the Fall of our First Parents."

Marxism or Christianity

In the preface to *Zero Hour and Other Documentary Poems,* D D Walsh calls Cardenal a Marxist-Christian poet. In his talk in Toronto, Cardenal himself endorsed this opinion. This raises questions which the epithet "Christian communist" does not. Whereas the communitarian roots of Christianity with an emphasis on social justice can have exactly the same immediate political projects as those of Marxist revolutionaries, their epistemological implications are very different. They spell out antithetical relationships between consciousness and the material world. This becomes a problem if Marxism is seen as a philosophy, a world view, a method of investigation of reality rather than solely as a political project: that is, if while discussing Marxism we talk not only of *The Communist Manifesto,* but also, for example, of *The German Ideology,* if we see *Capital* not only as an exposure of a particular type of exploitation, but as a method of exploring social formations. If such considerations are kept in mind one must come to a conclusion of an irreducible contradiction existing between materialist and idealist interpretations of the relations between the socio-historical world and forms of consciousness. One approaches reality radically differently depending on whether one believes that God created man or man created God.

Cardenal himself, neither in his talk in Toronto nor in his writing, seems to think there is any contradiction. While answering questions regarding his Marxism he equated the biblical notion of the Kingdom of Heaven on earth with the Marxist concept of the dictatorship of the proletariat. He also made statements such as "He saw that matter was good (a materialistic God)" and "Idols are idealism / While the prophets were professing dialectical materialism."

What could he have possibly meant by using such words as "materialism" or "dialectical materialism" in such ways and such contexts? This is not a usage that either materialists or idealists would accept because it robs words of their meaning in a consistent philosophical tradition.

It is politically and morally acceptable to say that Marxist politics and Christian ethics move towards the same goal. It is also true that the Nicaraguan "church of revolution" and the Marxists conceptualize history in terms of struggles of classes, struggles between oppressors and oppressed. Both reject exploitation and alienation and seek to establish a society of just distribution and development of creativity. Both consider basic needs rather than merit and at least in theory reject the division between mental and manual labour. So far so good. But things begin to stick at the epistemological divide.

The secularism of Marxism and the spiritualism of Christianity make it impossible for idealism and materialism to stand in for each other or be aggregated in a total world view. If anyone sees God as a figment of imagination, a product of idealist thought, that God cannot be seen as "a materialist God." It does make all the difference in the world whether we say that consciousness is determined by existence or the reverse.

It could be that if these two traditions of thought were spelled out and developed to their fullest ramifications they would actually have different practical or political implications, not just epistemological ones. It is my feeling that a "materialist" reading of the Bible would disempower the Bible itself of the type of moral force and revelatory character that Cardenal finds in it.

The other problem that emerges out of this attempt at what seems to me to be an unworkable synthesis is that the source of one's political and moral actions remains unclear and undifferentiated. This could pose a real problem if, for instance, one lost one's religious (idealist) motivations and had no secular ethics on which to proceed. This dilemma was posed a long time ago by Dostoevski in *The Brothers Karamazov,* in the question of Ivan, who said, "If God is dead, must not all things lose value and all actions including murder become permissible?" One need not cite such extreme examples except perhaps to point out the degree of confusion that such aggregation leaves one open to. Also, there are other possibilities that one must guard against. If, for instance, the people of Nicaragua see their revolution as a "Christian revolution," then a strongly divided pulpit, as suggested by the attitudes or dictates of the right-wing Cardenal Obando y Bravo of Managua, or of the Pope himself, could confuse the people and reassert reactionary trends. This could of course also weaken the participation of the clergy in general, and pose the problem of secession from the Roman church.

But even with these questions and reservations, one must revert to the position that the only revolutionary project that succeeds in any fundamental way must begin where people are. It must be a process that reclaims, regenerates and reconstructs the overall terrain of popular consciousness. The goal of social justice and the defence of the revolution from reaction and US imperialism have drawn the Nicaraguan people together, believers and nonbelievers alike; the coincidence of the will of the people has led to a convergence of political understanding and symbols. It is this great social movement that has spoken through the available ideology of Christianity. It is this that has radicalized Christianity.

NOTE. All quotations of poems of Ernesto Cardenal are translated by D D Walsh (*Zero Hour and Other Documentary Poems,* 1981); prose quotations are from *Christians in the Nicaraguan Revolution, Interviews with Margaret Randall,* translated by Mariana Valverde.

The Poetry of Dionne Brand

I am not a refugee
I have my papers
I was born in the Caribbean,
practically in the sea,
fifteen degrees above the equator,
I have a Canadian passport,
I have lived here all my adult life,
I am stateless anyway

(*Chronicles of the Hostile Sun*)

Historical novels have been much in vogue, much written about, but historical poems have a lesser visibility and are perhaps more difficult to write. In spite of the slogan that "the personal is the political," the two get written about in separate pieces, though sometimes joined by an "and." The sense of history that could lead to the fusion of both, that would lead to the writing of historical poetry, shows itself rarely. The ability to make history concrete by capturing the small, ordinary things of life along with a sense of broader historical actions is not to be found too frequently in English poetry, particularly on the land mass of North America. But of course it does happen that some poets do come along - dragging behind them the long chain of history, poets from groups who have been hidden in history such as women or black people, who institute themselves, their people, their history, centrally in the poetic universe. Dionne Brand, born in Trinidad, in Guaguyare (1953), immigrant to Canada, woman and black, is another such poet. To read her poetry is to read not only about her but also about her people, her identification with their struggles both in the metropole of Canada and the hinterland of the Caribbean.

It is this sense of history that makes the reading of Dionne Brand's poetry a dynamic experience. The reader is continuously struck by a set of complex movements that range from the past to the future, swiftly building connections between places, peoples, feelings and times. The reader just as much as the writer is required to be in many spaces all at once. But when one really thinks about it, to "be" actually does amount to being in that state of simultaneity. Both the content and the rhythm of her poetry suggest that she is always ahead of and trying to catch up with herself all at once. This amounts to catching up with the past to sense out the present mainly in order to seize the future. Her whole book of poems *Primitive Offensive* (1982) is just such an enterprise where delving deep into the ancestral past of slavery - "I will take any evidence of me even that carved in the sky" - she releases herself into the future:

. . . to be a bright and violent thing
to tear up that miserable sound
in my ear
I run
my legs can keep going
my belly is wind.

And the future is neither for Dionne Brand nor for any colonized, enslaved people one of a linear development to a genuine freedom, a happy place in the sun. The forces that once pillaged the world, structured the system of slavery, of colonialism, that now thrive on racism and neocolonialism, can push back the history of the people into new dark ages, new slaveries. Then once more the struggle begins, to emerge as a free people, through a populated time filled with cumulative experiences of victories and defeats. In her recent book of poems *Chronicles of the Hostile Sun* (1984) she remarks about the frustrations involved in describing such a process.

I'm sick of writing history
I'm sick of scribbling dates
of particular tortures
I'm sick of feeling the boot
of the world on my breast
my stomach is caving in and

. . . .
I'm sick of hearing chuckles
at my discomfort
I am sick of doing literacy work
with North Americans . . .

It is here that she deals most extensively with the contemporary Caribbean history, particularly in relation to the destruction of the Grenadian revolution by the US military invasion in October 1983 following the collapse of the government headed by Maurice Bishop.

Chronicles of the Hostile Sun synthesizes many experiences, many kinds of knowledge - an intimate knowledge of Trinidad where she grew up, her travels through the other islands and Nicaragua, and finally her involvement with the work of social and economic development of Grenada. This is where she worked for CUSO during the year of 1983 until the very moment of the US invasion. The poems in this volume show her understanding of the need for change in Third World countries as much as her profound sadness and anger at the world's wealthiest and most militarily equipped nation smashing the work and the hopes of 110,000 people inhabiting a 133-square-mile island. The memories and legacies of underdevelopment and slavery that the New Jewel Movement sought to eradicate returned in full swing dressed in US military uniform. In the division of the book into three sections, "Languages," "Sieges," and "Military Occupations," in poems such as "Diary - The Grenada Crisis," "October 25, 1983," "Night - Mt Pamby Beach - 25 March 1983," this invasion is anticipated, reenacted and denounced -

America came to restore democracy,
what was restored was faith
in the fact that you cannot fight bombers
battleships, aircraft carriers, helicopter gunships
surveillance planes, five thousand American soldiers
. . . .
You cannot fight it with a machete
you cannot fight it with a handful of dirt
you cannot fight it with a hectare of land free from bosses . . .

- and finally mourned in long poems such as "P.P.S. Grenada" or lines such as the following:

Maurice is dead
at 9:30 p.m. the radio
dream is dead
in these antilles
how do you write tears
it is not enough, too much
our mouths reduced,
informed by grief

windward, leeward
it is only October 19th, 1983
and dream is dead
in these antilles.

The bottomline of history is after all the lives of people, and by people is meant the poor, the oppressed of any society. The poem "Amelia" (written about her grandmother) is born out of the knowledge of their lives. Brought up by this woman as her child, as her "co-conspirator" the writer reproduces the daily grind, the reality of their world.

I know that lying there in that bed
in that room
smelling of wet coconut fibres
and children's urine
bundled up in a mound
under the pink chemille and cold
wearing sheets
you wanted to escape,
run from that room . . .

It becomes apparent as one reads through that volume that in this cramped, poor reality there is only room for one thing - change for the better. But this change will not be given, it must be taken through popular action or in terms of liberal advocacy of personal improvement. It is a collective change based on collective experience, and Dionne Brand describes such a world of shared experiences - of people, places and history. Here there are no strangers - "right away he knew me," "this old Carib" - and it is filled with "this charm of ours, this familial gesture." Little towns revisited "full of Jean Rhyses," slums with pigs, garbage and pot-bellied children, are all waiting for this collective change. And change seems suspended in the Caribbean sky, the "persistent sky" which in its orange and purple is a "vengeful motherfucker of a sky."

Dionne Brand's poetry expands to take in the Central American countries as well which are linked to Grenada with chains of oppressions and bonds of resistances. Her poetry sweeps through the panorama of El Salvador, Guatemala, Nicaragua, Honduras . . . all private estates of landowning gunmen who put their guns at the service of the United States and fatten from the leavings at their master's table. The country that she lingers over the longest is Nicaragua, the once-estate of Anastasio Somoza, struggling to survive a US seige carried out by the old ruling class and its military beneficiaries - now experts at international gangsterism. In the poem "Mount Pamby Beach," the life under such a constant seige is depicted forcefully. It points out the fact that the people of Nicaragua are not gun-happy, that they would rather be doing literacy or healthcare work or developing people's arts. But this opportunity has been denied to them; instead, what overhangs their life is

> this contra of a night
> [which]spilled criminals and machismo
> on our mountains
> fouling the air again
> eagle insignia-ed somocistas
> bared talons on the mountains of Matagalpa.

Not only this "night of the contras" initiated by external agents but also the allies of US imperialism receive their fair share of criticism from Dionne Brand. Prime Minister Seaga of Jamaica, Eugenia Charles of Dominica, and Tom Adams of Barbados are rewarded for their "internal initiatives."

> The OECS riding like birds on a cow
> led america to the green hills of St George's
> and waited at Point Salines
> While it fed on the young of the land,
> eating therir flesh with bombs,
> breaking their bellies with grenada launches

The rewards are further specified in

> What a privilege to hold a scotch
> simpering for the dollar bill
> from the CBI and USAID

for men "who know no more than the route to miami."

And finally back in Canada she encounters (and counters) the myths and lies that pervade the atmosphere about popular struggles in the Third World. For the referees of world socialism, who sit in the metropole and distribute points to the "correct" type of socialism in the Third World this is what she has to say:

Stay at home
where you are free to be a consumer
where you are free to walk the street
where you are free to demonstrate
where newspapers print what they like
even if they are lies
you will not know
truth is free to be fiction
counting is not an exact science

Chronicles of the Hostile Sun is not sure of what is to become of Grenada. It can only depict what is in the present, and it seems that much has been destroyed. The spectre of communism has been raised again and plugged into the cold-war channel which has all North America in its mind-numbing grip. But for the destruction of Grenada or the assassination of Walter Rodney the same lines can be applied:

and never, never for Walter
no words for Walter, no forgiveness,
everybit of silence is full of Walter.

The historical character of the *Chronicles* cannot be sufficiently understood without an exploration of an earlier volume of poems - *Primitive Offensive* (1982). Here the project is explicitly one of writing a historical poem, divided into several long cantos. But it is writing history with a difference since it involves locating herself at the heart of the history of all colonized peoples. Her own subjectivity is the starting point of her query, from which she branches back into the past exploring the construction of her own identity. To begin with, then, she is alone

When you decide
you are alone
when you dance
its on your own
broken face
when you eat
your own plate of stones
for blasted sure
you are alone

(Canto III)

But this aloneness is not an individualist, solipsistic enclosure; it is accompanied, filled with voices from the past, her ancestors, their experience of slavery. She invokes history in the following terms:

Ancestor dirt
ancestor snake
ancestor lice
ancestor whip
ancestor iron
ancestor slime
ancestor stick
ancestor iron
ancestor bush
ancestor ship
ancestor old woman, old bead
let me feel your skin . . .
(Canto III)

She has consented to inherit, to taste, no matter how painful and unsavoury all that her ancestors have left her. It is a legacy of blood, bitterness, death, rage, shit and tears as well as a militant love that rouses her to pick up as weapons two adjectives that her oppressors have labelled her and her people with - "primitive" and "offensive." She lifts these from the ongoing imperialist discourse and hurls them back to her oppressors as a call to war. Through an act of reinterpretation she has rid the word "primitive," for example, of its pejorative connotations and returned it to its meaning: the original, the essential and the basic. By reworking the word "offensive" back to its military sense she is now on the "offensive." No more strategy of retreat, the days of black defensiveness are certainly over.

Primitive Offensive is a book about war strategies and tactics, as much as about survival itself as a form of war against the oppressors. It is a book about countering the violence of domination in order to set right the violent world order created by colonization, slavery and imperialism. It is a poem, borrowing from Frantz Fannon, about decolonization, which cannot be waged without declaring and waging war - a war of liberation. Dionne Brand also declares her intention when she says:

I went to Paris
to where short-arsed Napoleon said,
"get that nigger Toussaint,"
Toussaint, who was too gentle,

he should have met Dessalines,
I went there to start a war
for the wars we never started
to burn the Code Noir
on the Champs Elysees
(Canto IV)

The war promises to be a long one, full of unpleasant surprises against which one must watch out:

Some solar-winged brutal contraption,
with another Columbus aboard
another Santa Maria perhaps
another De las Casas
another slavery
will surprise me
consorting with a boa constrictor.
(Canto V)

The world as it stands, produced by the long history of domination, is an inverted one. Both with the sword and pen the people of the colonized nations had been reduced to the status of objects, their subjectivity distorted or simply negated. And it is this inverted world that must be set back on its own base; the negation must be negated. It must be fought against - at all levels - social, economic and cultural. A struggle with the destructive Other is inevitable - but also there must be a project of retrieving or salvaging from the past whatever is relevant for now. Nothing that can be used will be thrown away. The task of some of the cantos in *Primitive Offensive* is to reassemble first, piece by piece, this lost world as one would the shards of ancient African pottery:

I posed over these
like a paleontologist
I dusted them
like an
archaeologist
(Canto III)

The way to accomplish this task is to go back in time, to seek out the lost steps back to the first moment of encounter with the whites, the moment of the Fall, as it were. The records of time are not to be found in the official textbooks of history or the archives. Rather, an appeal must be made to memory, to the oral tradition persistent among all people who are denied access to many tools of culture. So, an invocation is in order to an ancient spirit, who must speak in the sybilline, cracular tongue - to an ancient medicine woman. It is with this ancient woman that the young rebellious woman, the poet, must merge to know what really happened in history. This knowledge and acknowledgement of the past gives strength -"only when I remember I find myself."

The long nightmare of the past is then joined with the horrors of the present. A road runs straight through the old plantations into the present-day South Africa. The horrors of apartheid are laid bare in Canto XII:

a morning in Pretoria
a morning nervous and yellowish
its guts ripped out
and putrefying
stuffed back into its throat
The professor and the national party
and Botha
and Oppenheimer the diamond man
were skeptical about
the Bantu in Bothutapswana
good night from Pretoria . . .

And yet the tone of the poems, their message or messages to their readers, are not one of defeat but of courage, defiance and struggle. Even though the poet acknowledges her loneliness of an evening in an empty apartment in cities of the metropole, she also, and persistently, congratulates herself and others like her, because just to survive is an act of heroism. From this ability to survive, no matter on what - "I can eat stone and oil / I can eat barbed wire . . . I can grow fat on split atoms" (Canto V) - she projects courage and optimism. The Cuban revolution becomes the herald of a bigger revolution:

Havana twinkles
defiant, frightening
all the lights are on

(Canto VII)

Any discourse of *Chronicles of the Hostile Sun* and *Primitive Offensive* is incomplete without an assessment of their formal qualities. It is safe to begin by saying that they are a rare breed of poems - they are not short lyrics but mostly long poems; *Primitive Offensive* in fact is an attempt at an epic. The tradition of long poems, in the English language at least, seems to be on the wane. Epics are rarely attempted, and even more rarely, successful. The difficulty of writing long poems or narrative epiclike poems is obvious. They require much more than powerful feelings, or an ability to catalyze these feelings into strong, moving images. They require a coherent, well-articulated worldview and an ability to create a sustained narrative since one cannot possibly attend to a hundred pages or so of climactic moments. Both the books are successful in this blending of the imagistic, symbolic moments with narrative ones. In *Primitive Offensive* this requires an ability to create a general movement as well as an eye for details. The reader can almost taste, smell, see the gold and the blood of primitive accumulation in the pages of this book. Structuring the poem on different types of contradictions and inversions, she has kept a historical narrative in balance and located herself as a conscious subject within that frame. She has guided her reader through these turmoil-filled times with her sense of history, which moves from domination to revolution on through the agency of a conscious subject. And finally, as a craftswoman of the narrative, she has created and sustained the readers' interest with her strong sense of drama, through the use of historical details, vignettes, names and dates, of rituals and constellations of images, by frequently returning to the same image, as a signpost or an echo.

Chronicles of the Hostile Sun does not depend on the epic and the mythic qualities that characterize *Primitive Offensive*. In this set of poems, which must also be read as parts of a whole developing sequence (and can be read in single pieces as well) the narrative and the historicism take on some characteristics of reporting, recording, witnessing and commenting. The contemporariness of the poems demands this form above the chanting, incantating tone predominant in the earlier book. The poems in this book still become good or great poems due to a profound sense of the environment, or a conjunction of meanings worked up through the poet's own perception of the world, her own philosophy and politics. The long poem "P P S Grenada" is perhaps the best example of this. Describing the humble details of her everyday life in Grenada, that part of the landscape that she daily saw, this poem manages to convey the simplicity the peace that Grenada had before the invasion which are both intangible and irreplaceable. It is as though the writer was looking at photographs of a lost landscape. It is a recounting, a piece of history which is also a lamentation.

While *Chronicles of the Hostile Sun* is about the contemporary Caribbean, *Primitive Offensive* mainly about its historical past, *The Winter Epigrams* (combined in one volume with *Epigrams to Ernesto Cardenal in Defense of Claudia*) directly addresses Dionne Brand's experiences in Canada as struggles for survival in a frozen landscape. Seen through the eyes of an immigrant from the tropics, Toronto or Montreal come to life, shivering in the cold, a concrete desert, a social space constructed through racism. Here are two examples about winter in Montreal and Sudbury:

Snow is raping the landscape
Cote de Neige is screaming
writhing under
winter's heavy body
any poem about Montreal in the winter is pornography.
(Winter Epigram 17)

I've never been to the far north/cold,
just went as far as Sudbury,
all that was there was the skull of the earth,
a granite mask so terrible even
the wind passed huriedly,
the skull of the earth I tell you,
stoney, sockets, people
hacked its dry copper flesh.
I've heard of bears and wolves
but that skull was all I saw
it was all I saw I tell you,
it was enough
(Winter Epigram 18)

A small taut piece on racism is captured in a few quick strokes and the helplessness of the victim.

I had planned the answers all my life
rehearsed my "fuck offs"
practised my knee to the groin
decided to use violence;
now, leaving the train at Montreal,
gone!
all my rebuttals,

all my "racist pig"
nothing,
dried up!
iron teeth of the escalator
snickering like all of "them,"
my legs stiff as the cold outside,
my eyes seeing everything in blood,
a piece of cloth
a white mound of flesh atop
like a cow's slaughtered head,
emitting,
"whore, nigger whore!"

(Winter Epigram 51)

Alienation and long months of winter - and there seems to be no other season in the cities of the metropole - are negotiated by an underground life, surrounded by fetish objects from the past life and wry humour. The *Winter Epigrams* are quick parrys and thrusts at the enemy. They are, if such an expression can be permitted, guerrilla poems - a set of quick attacks and rapid withdrawals.

The second section of *The Winter Epigrams* entitled *Epigrams to Ernesto Cardenal in Defense of Caudia* assumes an ideal communicant in the Nicaraguan revolutionary poet and priest Ernesto Cardenal. Taking the Nicaraguan poet to task for his censoriousness about the average woman - the Claudias of this world - Dionne Brand proceeds to tell him a thing or two about the situation of women, about men, living and loving. But this is done humorously, whimsically, even lovingly and sometimes with downright craftiness. In "Epigram 27" for example she points out the loving though polemical nature of her poems to him - with humour:

Dear Ernesto:
I have terrible problems convincing
people that these are love poems.
Apparently I am not allowed to love
more than a single person at a time.
Can I not love anyone but you?
signed,
"desperate."

(Epigram 27)

About Claudia, whom Cardenal reprimands for her lack of rectitude, for selling herself to the foreigner, she has this to say:

> Some Claudias are sold to companies,
> some Claudias sell to street corners
> even debasement has its uptown,
> even debasement has its hierarchy.
> (Epigram 17)

or,

> poorest Claudia,
> to the love of a poet
> to the singing of a madrigal
> to the dictator's american shoes
> to the wall
> to the afternoon blossoms
> to the escape across unknown borders
> to the perfume of a freedom
> (Epigram 18)

The formal aspect of *The Winter Epigrams* and *Epigrams to Ernesto Cardenal* deserve a discussion of their own. They are wholly of a different nature than the books earlier discussed. Unlike the long and the medium-length poems, where ideas are discussed in their full ramifications, where images are grouped together in clusters, political viewpoints extensively developed, these poems are amused or serious experimentations with short, inconclusive but suggestive quick sketches. They are more in the nature of "thoughts" which may even be developed into fuller-sized poems. It is here also that we see some of the more so-called '"personal" poems of Dionne Brand - except that in each of these there is embedded a politics, an awareness of the dynamics of power. Patriarchy, or sexism to be precise, as a mode of social organization is penetratingly discussed in these short pieces. What appear from one point of view to be aspects of her own relationship with men, provide also a window into male-female relations in general. Personal accounts such as

> You're lucky I have a bad memory
> or I'd remember that red hot arrow
> in my ribs,

that feeling of turning to water,
I'd recollect that stupefied look I carried
on my face for three years,
all the signs, they said,
you're lucky I have such a bad memory
for names, faces
or I'd remember that I loved you
then.

(Epigram to Ernesto Cardenal)

acquire a social meaning, available to all members of patriarchically organized societies, when joined with the insights of the following kind:

Have you ever noticed
that when men write love poems
they're always about virgins or whores
or earth mothers?
How feint-hearted.

(Epigram to Ernesto Cardenal 32)

It is in this little book, through a small poem, that Dionne Brand writes about a new and feminist aesthetic. And again the personal, the political and the aesthetic work together, simultaneously and inseparably to talk about an idea and even to show what it looks like when actually put into practice. A thought on feminist aesthetic and an example, this poem deserves to be fully quoted:

Since you've left me no descriptions
having used them all to describe me
or someone else I hardly recognize
I have no way of telling you
how long and wonderful your legs were.
Since you have covetously hoarded all the words
such as "slender" and "sensuous" and "like a young gazelle"
I have no way of letting you know
that I loved how you stood and how you walked,
and forgive my indelicacy,
your corpulatory symmetry, your pensile beauty,
since you massacred every intimate phrase
in a bloodletting of paternal epithets
like "fuck" and "rape," "cock" and "cunt,"

I canot write you this epigram.
(Ars Hominis / the manly arts)

For centuries men have written love poems to women, coining words or phrases, or appropriating the language, that a mode of writing or description has developed which leaves very little room for women's subjectivity. It seems in the end writing antipoems to this tradition has to become the feminist mode, or at least a steady use of irony to undercut the tradition of a male-dominated aesthetic.

Talking of antipoems brings us to the topic of Dionne Brand's aesthetics - as far as they have developed up to now. Just as everyone, even the most "apolitical" person, does actually have some type of politics - no matter how deeply diffused or embedded this may be in the details of their daily life - so does everyone who writes any kind of poetry have a "poetics" or "aesthetics," which is their philosophy of arts and their selecting and crafting principle. Some writers are more self-conscious about this than others. Dionne Brand happens to be one of those poets who gives a great deal of thought to her own poetic projects as well as to poetry in general. Without crude functionalism, she even dares to ask the question "What is poetry?" - a question that is an anathema to the devotee of "pure" art. She even writes poetry about poetry, trying to answer her own question which declares a war with the pursuit of the "pure" art, or "culture" as understood by the elite. For her poetry is never "pure" nor an ornament nor an educated small talk carried on among the socially privileged. This is clear when one reads lines such as these:

Yes, but what else was done
except the writing of calming lines
except sitting in artsy cafes
talking artsy talk.
(Epigram to Ernesto Cardenal, 33)

Totally deploring "artsiness" Dionne Brand seems to want to write a kind of poetry which is "usable" in the business of everyday life, which is not transcendant over it. It is not set apart as a special activity but is one of the many things that people do to struggle through life, against forces that make ordinary everyday life impossible. Poets are not prophets in her eyes; poets are not even the revolutionary ones, the vanguards of revolutions. But wherever there is a struggle, she would accept that poets like others in society have a role to play - in their own particular way. This view of cultural activities, or poetry, is integral to the kind of politics that becomes evident in Dionne Brand's work. It is strictly speaking a politics of socialist reconstruction, and particularly the poem called "Anti-poetry" (*Chronicles of the Hostile Sun*) best captures the salient features of Dionne Brand's politics. Refusing to write poems which are like sending "self-addressed stamped envelopes" she is painfully aware of the limitations of poetry:

> Someone at a party
> drew me aside to tell me a lie
> about my poems,
> they said "you write well,
> your use of language is remarkable"
> well if that was true, hell
> would break loose by now,
> colonies and fascist states would fall,
> housework would be banned . . .

Even though "it is hell to keep a crow waiting" and to "hustle poems between the dancers and the drummers" she is reluctant to write poetry that is divorced from struggles and confusions or detached from the texture of daily life. In the last analysis her poetry is a form of struggle, and her poems are a witness to the struggles of others. It is this that joins profound compassion with militancy in her poetic work.

Andrei Tarkovsky: A Discourse on Desire and History

Tarkovsky's films are a discourse on space and time, which necessarily presuppose an active experiencing subject or consciousness (not a psychological "self"), in and through whom they become memory and history. History, memory, desire and nostalgia are therefore key words for thinking about what Tarkovsky is attempting to do. Now, if all this sounds a bit mysterious, it is not for that reason mystical or abstruse or self-indulgent. Since he must be considered in the entirety of his project, it is best to begin by discussing his first film, *Ivan's Childhood* (which Ritwik Ghatak considered "a major film in our time.")

"Ivan's Childhood," a short story by Vladimir Bogomolov, is a piece of history, in that it shows the transformation of a people and space during the time span of the Second World War and through the subject-consciousness of the child Ivan. It is Soviet history as it is the reclamation of the Second World War as fought by the Soviets. It is not an "official" history of names and dates of great generals and battles, but a "social" history - concentrating on a "social" memory of names, faces, events and experiences that were the everyday aspect in the Soviet Union of a war that cost twenty million people. And at the heart of these concentric circles of memory there is the story of a child Ivan, with his "personal" history, memory, of a village, a mother, a sunny afternoon, a bucket of cool water, all suddenly transformed, from out of the blue literally, by the dropping of a bomb. Space and time thus transformed have a different meaning and weight for Ivan now. What must he do? Who must he be? This charred and devastated space-time parallels twenty million lives. The child must struggle with his life, as Tarkovsky and others must struggle with him, since Ivan is their memory (their own childhood, boyhood, youth) of the war.

Ivan is an embodiment, but he is also a signal of history. He signals the childhood of the Soviet socialist republic itself - its continuities so abruptly cut. These thoughts are of course developed in the course of the overall narrative, but are also capsuled at the very beginning of the film by a few moments of cinema. The very first shot is that of a child looking at the sky through the tracery of a spider's web. He smiles and the landscape reflects that smile back to him in the glittering leaves, grass and the moving clouds. There is a wind - the child is swift - he runs headlong - he wants to fly. The camera flies out with his eyes, sweeps over the valley above which the child is playing. All this probably sounds corny and sweet from a verbal description; actually on screen it is too clean, sharp and swift to be so.

The movements of the child, the wind in the trees, etc. produce an effect akin to that of a dance, as though the camera is going through a whirl. This projective and friendly relationship with the natural space is followed by the same at a personal and social level. The camera narrows and creates a visual path, down which comes a woman who, small at first, grows larger, she has a bucket in her hand, her hair is tied up in a kerchief, she has a warm and friendly face, she is smiling. She stops by the child, presumably her son, puts down the bucket. The child kneels to have a drink, drinks, looks up at her and also smiles. The sky and her face are wide open, hospitable - and suddenly all changes. The camera swerves and swirls crazily. The faces, the sky, the landscape are all whirling, churning, cracking. The screen is fractured, shattered. Space cracks like a shelled stained-glass window, and its splinters fly out into a great blackness, and old, harmonious relations with space and time, with people and landscape, fly out with these. Ivan's time of grace has ended.

When this convulsion is over and the air ceases to tremble, the natural space is transformed, and so are the weather and Ivan. It is winter now, and the sky hangs like a lid over the earth, charred trees and houses rise out of the earth like warning hands. Ivan is dressed in winter clothes. He has the look of a wizened adult, he is alone and he steps into the cold waters of a marsh. There are bare trees surrounding him like silent threats, he creeps along, swims like a water rat, he is on his way to an army post, he has become like millions of other children a fighter for the Red Army. But again he is not for Tarkovsky a little war hero. Far from it.

Tarkovsky pours into this child all his regrets for violated childhood. Ivan is a combination of a terribly disturbed child and something of a little monster, a child possessed by the devil of war. He acts with the terrible cold precision of a war-hardened general when he outlines the enemy positions, producing a response of repulsion from the audience, which is immediately followed by compassion as he undresses, showing his emaciated child's body, or as he falls asleep at the table, is carried to bed by the older boy-soldier and puts his arms around his neck in sleep. In sleep memory takes its toll, Ivan can now step back from the coldness of shock to the sadness of memory. He has terrible nightmares. This child carries around in him a beheaded past, a murdered time as personal memory. His past and present have been torn apart, the war has put a knife through him. Neither can he integrate his whole past into the present, since he cannot go past that moment of destruction, nor can he unburden himself of it or discharge it.

Thus with *Ivan's Childhood,* Tarkovsky can be seen to establish his problematic alignment and realignment of space and time in and through experiencing subjects who must deal with history as dead or living memories. The problems of location and dislocation, of lives full of acts and being acted upon, a sense of self poised on the pin's head of time, the intermeshing of past and present generally known as making sense, getting on with life, spinning it out - are what Tarkovsky explores, not just film by film but also shot by shot in each film.

What keeps one going for Tarkovsky is either desire or its distortion - obsession. Dreams, longings, fantasies and obsessions propel his subject in its historical trajectory. The role of dreams is particularly crucial in that they are doubly revealing. They indicate the nature of the relationship with the past. Both the possibility of being locked into it and the desires that move one are present in them. They are inventories of time lived, death wishes to return to the past, or desires, which are forward-moving.

How one deals with the past, one's location in different mental and physical spaces, is further explored by Tarkovsky in the film *Solaris.* Based on a science-fiction novel by the Polish writer Stanislav Lem, *Solaris* is a more explicit exposition on the themes of memory, fantasy and desire. Here, released from the constraints of commonsense realism, Tarkovsky removes the subject from the planet earth, with its positivist-technological-linear rationality, from a functionalist space to the planet Solaris, whose substrate is a living (cellular) plasmatic jelly which can produce endless formations. Here, in relative isolation, stepping outside earthtime as it were, the subject - a scientist-psychiatrist - watches/acts with his colleagues, who are enthralled by, are in the throes of their own realized fantasies and desires. It is all the more horrific and anxiety-provoking because the people have no real direct access to their desires, and in fact have not conceded the reality of such things as desires and the unconscious on account of their behaviourist-rationalist frames of thought. The planet however has the property of realizing these as well as memory - continuously making past present and thereby forcing the subject to come to terms with it. The difference between the authentic subject and the others is that he is not afraid of either his past or this endlessly formative planet. Unlike his "rational" colleagues, he does not barricade himself into his laboratory, dying of slow emaciation and insanity.

Indeed he becomes so attuned to this world of figurative fantasy, he realizes so clearly the positive role of desire-fantasy, seeing it as the antithesis of insanity, discontinuity, isolation and arrested growth, that he leaves his mission unaccomplished.

He returns to earth a disgraced scientist but a wiser and sadder man. The question he poses for us is - if the authenticity of one's subject status is in an interaction with one's personal and social space and time, and if the creative moments of self-knowledge are inscribed in the hieroglyphs of fantasies and desires, and if our distorted desires parade before us in horrific formations, must we destroy our creative, figurative ability, or instead inquire what in our space-time relationships produces terrible fantasies and forms of distorted desire?

The creative unconscious in *Solaris* is shown to be deeply social; and it is not only a source or destruction and distraction, but also the capacity of existing as a subject in history. Barricading one's self from history - no matter how horrible the historical formations may be - and escaping into a positivist functionality/rationality (and inventing the word "irrational" to label all that this "rational" frame cannot comprehend) is actually opting out of history, that is to say, ceasing to "be." This being, which requires a going beyond the surface and the immediate, is "visionary" and Tarkovsky rescues "vision" from the monopoly of the mystics. Throughout his work and in this film he counters "vision" with the shallow realism of "calculation."

This visionary element, grounded in authentic desire, is also the centre of *Stalker,* whose subject is a stalker of dreams. He guides two members of the intelligentsia, a scientist and a writer to a room in an out-there "zone" situated in what appears to be the debris of an atomic world war, where one's deepest desires/dreams come true. As in *Solaris,* the space out-there is a way to here and now, its out-thereness being a result of our lack of access to ourselves, our core of desire and history. The metaphor of discovery of space, either in Tarkovsky or the science fiction writers Boris and Arcady Strugatsky, is not one coding a "domination" of nature, but that of a simultaneous voyaging out into the unknown of nature and a voyaging into one's self, memory and desire.

In both films the (middle-class) intelligentsia fear to face their dreams/fantasies. In *Solaris* the scientists either closet themselves with their dreams as with their secret vices, or hide in their labs from the figures of their desire, who stalk the corridors of the spaceship in search of them. In *Stalker* the scientist and the novelist, after all the strain and tension of getting there, refuse to go into the room, and risk their dreams/wishes coming true. But here there is also a great difference. They have agreed to be led by someone who is in fact familiar with the "zone" - who is free of personal ambition and has nothing to ask of the room. It is also worthy of notice that this guide, the Virgil of the intelligentsia, is a working-class man. This journey into authenticity/desire is a joint enterprise, not a lonely, solipsistic vision. In *Solaris,* where there is no guide, no related "other," no companionship, there is only a member of the intelligentsia, sensitive and discerning and terribly lonely in the isolation of his knowledge. His Solaris is a planet of one.

In *Nostalgia* these preoccupations are assayed in images. In this film the subject is not removed from the everyday earth to another planet or a "zone." Remnants of self-perpetuating machines from the Second World War, or the abstraction of a plasmatic planet are no longer needed. There are the bare bones of a story, some stations of thought, some encounters, pivoted (as in the other two films) on the time-worn theme of a journey. The planet is definitely the planet earth, the location of the subject is Italy in peacetime, and the subject is a Russian writer who has come to reconstruct the experience of an expatriate Russian poet who came to Italy in the last century. The subject, the experiencing, knowing self, at this juncture of space and time is like the medieval Everyman, a compound figure. The others around him embody stages or parts of him. Sosnosky, the nostalgic dead poet, the biographer himself, and Domenico, a recluse who locked up his family for years in a vain attempt to protect them from the world, together constitute a totality of ways of being. All of them must come to terms with the world and themselves. Memory, history, the other/others, the world are therefore points at stake. A journey must be made to understand these, and to be an authentic subject in relation to these.

The journey motif in *Nostalgia* or in other films of Tarkovsky is used in ways similar to that of Dante in *The Divine Comedy* - a road travelled through all painful, unacceptable things, through suffering, into a vision, though not of beatitude. As in Dante, the writer here is directed at each stage of his journey. His first guide is the woman (in Dante it is carnal pleasure) who brings him to the glimpse of hell - a sulphur spa - where the poet Sosnosky spent some time. Consumed with memories of Russia, unable to come to terms with the present, Sosnosky (and the writer) haunted these mist-filled pools with floating heads, which seem to be the visuals for Dante's denizens of the inferno. At this point, due to a struggle regarding sexuality, the woman leaves the poet. Though she is unable to comprehend his quest, she leaves only after she has helped him reach Domenico, the recluse.

The writer and Domenico are both self-imprisoned, the writer locked in memories of life in Russia, and Domenico in his fear of the world. Neither the writer nor Domenico are willing to engage with anything or anybody. The memories of both are of a lost world - of a world that is left behind because people must move in and through time; memories of an unrepeatable world haunt them. This time in the mind, this memory, because walled-in or cut by dislocation in space (another country), has been made to step outside of history. It is in no way capable of being integrated with the present due to a particularly frozen character ascribed to them, and as such can only become obsessional. Lived in such a manner, these memories cannot become the roots of identity, but its prison - the arrestation of development of the subject.

Through the first half of the film, in spite of many outdoor shots (many of landscapes of memory), the screen creates a sense of inertness, heaviness and claustrophobia. Shadows fill the writer's world, and they take on a solidity that the "shades" of Hades do in Dante - more menacing than anything that is so-called "real." The writer's hotel room becomes a darkened cavern, filled with shadows and little hints of light, just as his mind is, and outside it rains endlessly - memory and desire. The bed he sleeps on, as though dead, becomes a ship that ferries him into never repeatable yet endlessly recurring dreams. The writer, however, must dream them, must go through them and comprehend his own dislocation and arrestation as did the subject in *Solaris,* or the trio in *Stalker.* This of course is not easy. In all three films, facing the past (and thus the self) is dangerous, full of treachery; any wrong move - dishonesty, illusion or repression - will lead to death or insanity. The symbolic act of self-immolation of the recluse that the writer imagines is a violent leap of faith into an otherwise unknown, unaccustomed world - a recluse's self-destructive first contact.

Domenico cannot do more than that, the light he carries within him becomes a conflagration that destroys him. The poet must go on further, must complete Domenico's journey, keeping alive the little candle's light. In the act of walking through the sulphur pool, the writer completes Domenico's task. The task completed, the film ends - with an image in which the Italy of now, with its broken church, missing roof, the altar and the windows, cradles in its centre the landscape of the writer's obsessional dream. Surrounded by the sunlight of Italy, it snows in the landscape of Russia. The past and the present are both here. Then and now, involved in this complex image, established Tarkovsky's truth. It seems as though the truth is not that each is true in its own way and added together, but that they are together a new image, a new truth. It is not truth in the sense of "fact," but a construction of a comprehensive, intelligent consciousness. It is this interest in reality constructed by consciousness, the mind's way of comprehending the historically concrete, that Tarkovsky explores - which may be taken for "faith" or the "religiosity" of his work. There is an element of "belief" involved in this facing of the self, the past and the other; a courage also that is esentially for entering the room of dreams. It is difficult and perhaps redundant to call it religious.

After all, the church in *Nostalgia* has no altar, no divinity guides the writer's path. All must be the work of the writer - the "faith" he has is the conjoining of many spaces and times. It is that act of carrying the little light through the wind. The little candle, an ancient symbol in many cultures, illuminates much about both the fragility and persistence of life and visions. But a close scrutiny yields the knowledge that history - the labyrinth of space and time - through which a subject must walk - is for Tarkovsky a matter of mystery, not mysticism. The "illumination" is the work of the subject, not a free gift - that is, a "revelation."

Tarkovsky is neither orthodox nor original in the methods he chooses for conveying his vision. Unashamedly, blatantly he falls back on time-worn symbols and the literature of vision. Obvious allusions to Dante (e.g. Domenico to the writer: "Pay them no heed, these creatures, just walk on."), cliches and verities, techniques of symbolist and surrealist art are all serviceable devices for him. To anyone familiar with St Augustine's *City of God,* the walk with the candle could resurrect the sentence: "There is yet a little light un-put-out in man. Let him walk - let him walk - so darkness overtake him not." easter night processions with candles also perhaps come to mind for Christians.

But even outside of the religious context, this symbolism, as used by Tarkovsky, is charged with an appropriately secular significance. It rings true to all who are concerned with the problem of memory and self, who realize that "nostalgia" is different from one's ordinary, everyday memory, that "nostalgia" is dead memory, an experience that has been wrenched out from the flow of time/space/self interactions. It is in fact a reified, frozen moment, it overhangs people's lives like the four walls of a prison. These dislocated, decontexted memories with their seeming autonomy prevent people from standing firmly on their past in order to reach out to the future. Memory as such, as distinct from this reification, is not at all a problem. It is in fact the core of "social" being - the only way of being with which individuals are privileged.

A Western audience's discomfort with Tarkovsky, despite the approval of his "defection" from the Soviet Union, is perhaps due to the habits of narrative and forms that we are being inculcated with. It seems as though unabashed seriousness about matters such as a subject's relationship with history, the problem of social construction of memory and desire are not prime film material, at least not in that sort of unironic way. "Philosophical" issues, if they must be raised, must be differently narrated. But Tarkovsky derives from the long tradition of the "serious" Russian artist, where no apology is made for length (e.g. Tolstoy, *War and Peace*) or depth (Dostoevsky, *The Brothers Karamazov*). Soviet socialist realism notwithstanding, from Chernyshevsky, Goncharov, Tolstoy, Dostoevsky, Vertov, and Eisenstein to now there may be a greater continuity than we realize. Whether one likes Tarkovsky or not, one has to realize that his work is not the self-indulgence of a liberal but a serious discourse on man at the axis of space and time. But are are we ready for it? Do we want to think about history, personal or otherwise? Are we ready to enter the room of dreams?

Evenings Out: Attending Political Theatre in West Bengal

Nothing is irrelevant to society and its affairs. The elements that are clearly defined and can be mustered must be presented in relation to those that are unclear and cannot; these too have a place [in our theatre].

BERTOLT BRECHT, *The Messingkauf Dialogues*

The experience of theatre starts long before the curtain rises and the play begins. Our theatre exists in the world in which we live, and our theatre experience, shaped by that world, rises from it and returns to it. The world of theatre is not sufficient unto itself. Neither art nor its experience is a separate reality.

Towards the end of the 1930s, and especially since the foundation of the Indian People's Theatre Association (1943), there developed among the middle classes of Bengal a political theatre movement which was centred in Calcutta. This movement, which originated and continued to develop in the context of a growing Marxism and communism in India, created a new tradition of explicitly political theatre which has become dominant in non-commercial theatre in West Bengal and thrown up figures who are considered the most important theatre producers of West Bengal in the postindependence (1947) era. The playwrights see their theatre work as a form of conscious intervention and a part of the overall revolutionary process, and as such they are entirely preoccupied with representations of class and class struggle. My attempt here has been to describe the audience of two actual performances of such plays. These two evenings out are meant to capture the cross-currents of social relations which structure the audience's experience of the main-stream political theatre in Calcutta, West Bengal.

The two descriptions are meant to reveal certain features which are crucial both to the construction and study of this theatre. If we look at them closely, it becomes apparent that they arise in relation to an ex-colonial capitalist economy and a bourgeois socio-cultural environment. They display certain dramatic forms and social-political relations which are peculiar to these realities. On the one hand, we have the direct political intention of the playwright-directors, on the other, equally political, though indirect and unstated, the pressure of the existing social relations and dramatic conventions which shape the representational efforts. These mediational aspects of theatre production shape indirectly the final politics of this theatre, as they also shape the way reality is represented.

An Evening in an Auditorium

It was 5:30 in the afternoon. I was waiting at a bus stop going to see a play that started at 7 p.m. The bus stop, as usual, was very crowded, and each time a bus came people rushed to get in. I missed three buses, then spotted a taxi, hurled myself into it before it quite stopped, and arranging clothes, bag, hair, said, "Academy of Fine Arts please."

We sped through streets filled with vehicles and people. The crowd of buses, cycles, rickshaws, cars, taxis and pedestrians parted and swerved and made room for each other. Through the taxi windows I looked at the houses that we passed by - two to four storeys high, old, shoulder to shoulder, every balcony jammed with people, clothes drying. They could all do with repairs and a coat of paint. And the ground floor of each had a small or a middle-sized shop. Shopkeepers sat on chairs at the doorways. No electricity because of "load-shedding" - a term for eight to ten hours of power cut every day. Small kerosene lamps and big petrol lamps were being lit. Some better-off shops had private electrical generators roaring away. Hot and humid weather. Clothes stuck to the body. Everywhere on the walls people had put their politics in bold letters, colours and images. Bright red hammer-and-sickle signs with "Vote Communist Party of India (Marxist) for a better life" confronted the amputated right hand of Congress (Indira) raised in benediction. The taxi sped through this towards the Academy of Fine Arts.

As we went towards the Academy the street changed. Sidewalks had walking room and the stalls and vendors had disappeared. The houses were big, set back within gardens. They had high walls, topped with pieces of broken glass and often guards in khaki uniforms sat outside the gates, kneading tobacco in their palms. Parks were filled with flowers, not hovels and clothes drying on bushes. The poor featured now in some service roles and every house had electricity, meaning a private generator. The few shops there featured expensive goods. We passed by the Calcutta Club, with a Victorian fat-bottomed opulence, and the housing complex of the American consulate with its twelve- to fourteen-feet-high walls topped with electrified wire. Now I had reached the edge of the huge "maidan," an open stretch of parklands and trees, containing Fort William, the race course, and the golf course. Rising out to a sea of dark green foliage, against a shell-pink sky, was the cupola of the Victoria Memorial Museum. The angel on the dome, now a silhouette against the evening sky, raised her head to blow her trumpet.

There it was, the Academy of Fine Arts, across the tree-flanked street, a place of new culture facing the old culture of colonial India. It stood among a cluster of what could be called "cultural buildings," such as the Nehru Memorial Museum, Calcutta Information Centre and Ravindrasadan, a huge auditorium, complete with fountains, murals, mirrors, red carpets, chandeliers and plush seats, named after the nation's poet, Rabindranath Tagore. The grounds of this building are going to be shared by the West Bengal government's new cultural complex. To the left of the Academy there is the huge neogothic Anglican Cathedral of St Paul's. The grounds are laid out sumptuously and spires of the church soar out of a huge clump of trees.

The Academy of Fine Arts is a two-storey building but relatively tall, dove grey, with brick-red trimmings and terra-cotta friezes. It occupies a large compound filled with tall flowering bushes and flower beds, with a fountain at the entrance and old, massive trees beside the high wall that surrounds it. It has both an auditorium and an art gallery. In the left section of the grounds there is a small two-storey bungalow, which belongs to Lady Ranu Mukherji, the owner, who has taken the private initiative to create a public space for art.

In front of this cultural edifice I got out in a hurry. I had neither booked nor bought my ticket, but my hope was that a few university teachers that I know, who are also theatre critics and writers, would have got here earlier and bought them. I rushed over to the box office windows and found that indeed my friends had bought the tickets, and what is more, the director, who is a friend of some of us, was standing there. With my friends there were three men, whom I knew slightly, who are novelists and critics. I greeted these people. The director said that he had to go in, to put on his costume and make-up. He was both the lead actor and the writer of this play. As we walked towards the entrance of the auditorium, we ran into many people we knew. They were all somehow connected with writing, teaching and theatre. The editor of the well-known left theatre magazine, *Group Theatre,* was with us. He stopped every few steps to chat with someone. At the three other box office windows which sell tickets for shows on other days, people were buying advance tickets. I passed by the greenest of lawns strewn with sculptures that looked ancient and uncanny in the evening light. I overheard conversations about a film by a young left film maker, about the new German cinema, about bits of politics. There were a few women walking past me, who looked as though the chauffeured cars waiting outside the gate belonged to their families. The theatre producers were not themselves rich.

As I stood there thinking, waiting for the first bell to go, someone tugged the end of my sari. I looked around and saw this young person, an urchin, he could be called, a little vendor's boy, who said eagerly, "Didi (older sister) do you want tea or coffee?" He was a great contrast to the well-clad people who bustled around the place or stood in small groups, the men smoking. He was very thin, contrasting with the pudgy softness of many of the others, his skin lacked their smoothness. It was dry and ashen-looking. He was very short, probably small for his age, and his collar bones stood out sharply. Around his young birdlike scrawny neck he wore a sweat-soaked thread from which hung a copper amulet. His large eyes stood out in the dark small face like two pale shells on a dark surface. Now he was projecting a great intensity through them. He was eager, expectant and pleading. He varied his address for me and said, "Buy some coffee, or fanta or thumbs-up, mem sahib." The word "mem sahib" was originally used as an appellation for white women, and by now applied to Westernized and upper-class Indian women. "You think I am a mem sahib?" I asked. "No, didi," he said, "but I try everything. Do you or your friends want tea or coffee?" I asked him to bring four coffees and two teas. He ran up to the snack bar, filled with covered boxes of snacks and kettles of tea and coffee. A man as thin as the boy, with tight lips and oiled hair, stood at the bar. He looked better off than the boy, with a pair of intact trousers and a greying and stained shirt. He and another similarly dressed man standing by him, unlike my companions, were not "gentlemen," bhadralok. They were only "men." When I went to pay he spoke to me in the honorific "you" and I should have used the familiar form. His teeth were stained with pan (betel nuts and leaves). The men surveyed this theatre scene and culture-seeking people calmly - only interested in their business.

"Have you seen this play?" I asked.

"No," said the thin man, "we don't go to shows here."

"Why?" I persisted. "Too expensive?"

"No," he said rather curtly. But his companion was more loquacious. "These things are for you people, for the gentlefolk. Don't understand what's going on, what's being said."

"More fun," said the boy.

"How do you know what it is like if you haven't seen it?"

"Oh, we've been inside once or twice, and he," pointing to the boy, "goes in with messages all the time. But why do you want to know all this, mem sahib?"

"Oh, just curious. Never mind. Here's your money."

His palm was broad and the line of fortune had been rubbed out by callouses, his nails were dirty and broken. I could hear the first bell. I walked towards the entrance, past the mural and the statues. The play, called *Jagannath,* was about to begin. It was about a landless peasant who had become inadvertently mixed up with nationalist politics. The poster at the door showed a man in a torn undershirt, thin, with sharply pointing collarbones, not unlike the vendors themselves.

Unlike the outside, the air-conditioned auditorium was cool and dry. I sat in the second row of an auditorium which, including the balcony, holds 850 people. Before the lights went out I looked around at the audience. They were people like myself, genteel and middle class - no flair, no flash. Educated men and women - office-workers, teachers, writers, critics - "cultured" people, who have been the backbone of Bengali culture since the last century. People of modest or even low income who attend political theatre - plays about the peasantry. The same people would also go to plays because they were "art" rather than "entertainment." It was their patronage that developed the non-commercial theatre of Calcutta from the early 1940s. They had some understanding of the noncommercial theatre's project of connecting public education and art. Many of them had come straight from work. They had briefcases with them. The women wore no make-up. They wore nice cotton saris, not silk, and did not have many ornaments. They were "decent" Bengali women. They were probably among those in the cities and the countryside of Bengal who had voted the communist-led left front state government into power, and helped to maintain it there. Plagued by inflation and unemployment, it made sense that they would be there, trying to understand the role of the peasantry in Indian politics. With them I was here waiting for the curtain to rise.

And the curtain did not rise as the lights went out. We sat in a pitch darkness which only auditoriums can have, and people waited expectantly. Someone said, "Oh bother, it's load-shedding here too!" People coughed and fidgeted and a voice, over the amplifying system, very clearly enunciated the following lines - "Jagannath Das has been hanged by the British government as a terrorist. We will now observe a minute's silence to show our respect for him." The voice had a magical effect, the audience stopped fidgeting and whispering. Without expectation, even those who had not realized that this was the beginning of the play fell into a deep silence. The minute seemed endless, and having produced the necessary attention, the lights at the foot of the curtain slowly went into action and the curtain began to rise. At this point we noticed a man standing on the outer edge of the apron of the stage. In a prisoner's striped clothes he stood, framed by a circle of light, isolated by that light as though in his prison cell.

The stage had minimum properties. A raised platform at the back with a sacrificial block that is used in temples, a barred door on the right-hand corner, and a door frame on the left side, that was all. A little group of three or four men had formed in the corner of the stage. They discussed the British government's curious choice of victims in its attempts to repress the freedom struggle in India. Why hang Jagannath as a freedom fighter, they asked? Born in the lowest caste, a cowardly, landless peasant, something of a slave and a buffoon, an opportunist who knocked on any door, including that of an informer. Why was he hanged in an exemplary punishment by the British state as a political activist? This great unknown, the poorest of the rural poor, how had he become mixed up with our nationalist politics? Who was he really, this Jagannath Das? - asked the most militant of the freedom fighters, when one of the other men stepped out of the group and came to the very edge of the stage.

Facing the audience, talking to them directly, he said, "I have known Jagannath since his childhood. He is from my village . . . " The rest of the play was an attempt to answer the question of the freedom fighter - not however as an individual's biography, but rather as a display of a set of social relations specific to the lives of such people as Jagannath. It was interesting that it was the middle-class ex-freedom fighter who had initiated this long-awaited question about the peasantry. The play was more an exploration of a problem, through extremely fragmented narrative techniques, than a story. The story, if one can call it that, was inspired by *The True Story of Ah-Q* by the Chinese novelist Luh Suhn.

The people sat, as though mesmerized, throughout the play. Combining different acting styles, using a great deal of the lead actor's body, using Grotowsky-style physical acting - the play came to a conclusion when Jagannath slowly climbed up to the steps of the gallows, smiled at the audience, took up the noose and put it around his neck. The audience broke into a thunderous applause. All through the play they had been very quiet, there were no children, there was no frequent getting up and coming back.

During the break I sat outside and smoked with my friends. They felt that it was a very well-done play, very well acted, with evenly paced movement from scene to scene, but that the episodes with women characters smacked of sentimentality and the acting style of Bengali commercial cinema. There were also questions about the representation of the nationalist movement. People sat and chatted in small groups or stood around smoking. When the bell rang they trooped back in and some people, returning to their seats just as the curtain rose, lowered themselves so as not to obscure the view of the stage. Altogether it was a theatre-trained, or rather an auditorium-trained audience.

What, I asked myself in my journal, happened that evening between me/us, the audience and the stage? The play, having begun in this abrupt way, drew us right in, but again pushed us back by using the stage in a stylized, nonnaturalistic fashion. The groupings/blockings on the stage, the enactment in sketches of the main formative episodes of Jagannath's life, the expansion of each of them into a scene, all made it apparent to us that this was theatre, not life - that this was a problem, not a biography. And yet, and for that reason perhaps, the play carried us relentlessly to the end. The director was playing with both what is probable and what is possible. The multiplicity of enacted possibilities, and not only the excellent acting (particularly that of the director and lead actor Arun Mukherji), outlined some of the roles for peasants in politics and the relationship between them and the middle class. Class became palpable as a social relation in each episode between this cowardly, abject, yet imaginative and angry peasant and his superiors and equals. I, and all the other members of the audience, sat at the edge of our seats and saw ourselves and our ancestors, members of the middle class and landed gentry, and we saw in Jagannath a man with whom our contact through centuries has been only through exploitation and servitude.

We saw him as one of our silent servants, the squatting obedient voter or the bussed-in rally-attender, the rickshaw puller who won't meet your eyes, the street vendor who sells roasted maize, the coolie at the railway station whose back is permanently bowed from carrying massive weight. Many faces, many functions - all of servitude. His body itself is humble, thin, straining at each muscle, like a weak buffalo harnessed to a heavy cart. And we also saw his anger - which we glimpse in the ferocious struggle with the coolies at the railway station, the cold ruthlessness with which they will cheat you, the angry eyes of the rickshaw puller when you, by mistake, don't give him the union rate, the servant as he stands at bay with his eyes smouldering in front of the master unable to balance his account because he can't count.

Jagannath's ineffectual fantasies of power, his cheerful fantasy massacre of the landlords, showed the sleeping, smoking volcano in the peasant's mind. What are we, the middle class, supposed to do? After all we do want to engage in a revolutionary communist movement, and with people like him, about whom our knowledge is at best incomplete, mostly inaccurate. It became clear that this man's servitude will not make him a valid political agent, but his anger will. But that anger is directed towards our class, us as employers of servants, users of the familiar pronoun towards all lower classes, us the urban educated middle class - rational and civilized. If we want to be part of his politics, or more accurately want him to be part of ours, then we must learn to deal with his anger and our fear. And here we were - actors, director, playwright, audience - all middle class, asking and trying to answer, without a peasant audience or peasant actors or any form of input from the peasantry - what is a peasant's state of political consciousness? What can be his contribution to a revolutionary movement and how must the middle-class leader of a movement conceptualize the peasant? We have the right and the necessity to ask the question, but do we have the ability to answer it? Throughout the evening my head buzzed with questions. The play had a Brechtian quality to it and had made us think. It also had a lyrical touch to it, a sadness that moved us. For me, there was also the sentimentality and lack of clarity about women's roles, which bothered me a great deal. I was moved, critically stimulated, irritated - all at once. Who is representing whom, this was my main thought or concern. After the play was over we went to the "green room." In the lighted mirrors, I saw the illusion being stripped. Old torn shirts, dirty dhotis were replaced by trousers and "bush" shirts or punjabis. Eyes and faces with pancake make-up, shadow and eyeliners were being rubbed off with vaselined rags. Another face was emerging from the peasant's face - that of the Bengali bhadralok, a babu, a middle-income, genteel gentleman. The vendor's boy whom I met earlier in the evening was now serving tea busily. Arun, the director, lead actor and playwright - my old friend - met my eyes in the mirror and smiled. "How was it?" was the question that came next. A man's answer silenced me: "It was amazing what you did," he said, "such a typical peasant. You were more authentic than what we see nowadays. Now they are all gentlemen, you know, with their bikes, watches and transistors!"

What do they mean, his words? From where did he know what a peasant "typically" is?, I thought as I sat in the bus on my way back home. This evening had given much to me, to all of us. It was a very complex set of thoughts and emotions that had stirred up in me. What went into our responses? What shaped the theatre? How could we see clearly into what we call our experience?

An Evening in a Field

8 March 1983 - Chetana is putting on a production of Brecht's version of Gorki's *Mother*. So we have a production which moves from Gorki (Russian) to Brecht (German) to Bentley (English) to Arun Mukherji (Bengali). It was part of a week of festivities - part of the National Convention of the student wing of the Communist Party of India, Marxist (CPI(M)).

It was taking place in the open grounds near a college where the conference was being held. Something must be said about this locality (Garia district), both sociologically and politically, if we are to place the audience for this theatre. The people living here had been among those displaced by the partition of Bengal at the independence of India (1947). The 1970-71 disturbances in Bangladesh brought in a fresh spate of people. They were either indigent or had very little money, they were of petty bourgeois origin, some urban some rural, and they were not able to find a secure niche for themselves in the economic organization of the new country. They were "gentle folk" (bhadralok) however, and unable to do work of the working class. Later there were others who moved into the area - businessmen, professionals, and others who were forced by inflation to move out of the inner city. Now it is a densely populated area with isolated pockets of well-to-do people - with small factories and businesses. Once itself a hinterland for Calcutta's markets, supplying vegetables and fish, it still supplies maidservants and day labourers who come from the dispossessed rural people and the outer edges of this area. This combination of the somewhat educated threadbare gentry, generations of clerical workers and the working class (with peasant traits) make up the people that are the CPI(M)'s constituency. It was for their entertainment and edification that the play was going to be put up.

At six o'clock I appeared at the venue. The organizers had fenced off a big field where the local youth usually play soccer. They had constructed a wrought-iron gate decorated with red flags with the hammer-and-sickle. On either side of the gate, on two sides of the road, were tea stalls, push-cart vendors of all kinds selling fried chick peas, ground nuts, cigarettes, etc. Extending from either side of the gate, hugging the bamboo fence were display stalls, or exhibition booths as they were called. They exhibited different aspects of rural and urban development and public welfare undertaken by the left front government. The stalls displayed photographs taken at different sites and some gave information about different types of small technology used in agricultural and urban projects. There were also booths with art work by the Democratic Writers and Artists' Front - which is a coalition of creative/cultural producers with left/progressive sympathies - in particular CPI(M)-related. These booths were arranged in circles, each touching the other, forming an inner wall - leaving in the middle a circular open space which was supposed to be the auditorium. Red flags on high bamboo poles flew everywhere and there were several huge microphone speakers tied atop other high poles. The place was teeming with people - the microphones were blaring out songs of struggle from the Indian Peoples Theatre Association (IPTA), and a stage beautifully draped with blue cloth had been constructed at the north end. The stage was quite high, about four feet above the ground, presumably to be visible to a crowd of about five thousand people.

The ground, which had been walked bare in the course of the last few days and was hard as rock with packed, dry clay, was now covered with cotton rugs. There were no chairs - as is common with large outdoor performances. Many people were already sitting in clumps, smoking. Everywhere people talked, shouted. The air was full of dust. A vast movielike sunset in purple and orange overhung this scene. A Bengali version of "At the Call of Comrade Lenin" played on the microphones while the actors prepared themselves behind the scene.

The audience was probably three to four thousand in number and seemed to be mostly women and children. A great many seemed to be of working-class origin. One could tell this by the way they dressed - either wearing their saris in the way women wear them in villages, or wearing them in the urban style but too high. Tucked in the wrong places, they lacked that impractical, flowing, graceful touching-the-ground look of the middle/upper middle classes. The women looked thin (middle-class people are sort of plump), angular, awkward by middle-class standards. Their hair was well oiled, slicked back, the vermillion put on thick and bright in the part in the middle, they had a big red spot in the centre of the forehead and wore lots of plastic, imitation gold jewellery. They had on their best clothes and had dressed their children too in bright clothes with hair tightly braided. The men who sat or stood about dressed in the usual pants - frayed at the edges, cheap - also with hair oiled and slicked back, seemed lower middle class, and working class. Some men were in lungis which no gentleman would wear out for an evening. There seemed to be a student youth population floating about - of threadbare gentility, most likely unemployed. They came from the local "refugee" families. CPI(M) has a very strong base among this section of the population. But the majority of the people, while generally positive to CPI(M), and certainly not afraid of communism, were there because it was their neighbourhood, and every evening there were songs, movies, plays and speeches from the different departments of government and the Party.

The directors of the play asked me to keep an ear open to audience reaction. They had distributed a questionnaire at some previous shows at the Academy of Fine Arts, but since the method of a questionnaire-based opinion survey seemed to make no sense here, and since he had no part in the play, Arun Mukherji decided to plant himself and some of us in strategic places to talk with people during the break and after the play. So about six of us - members and friends of the group - spread ourselves among the audience. I found myself sitting in a group of women - two or three old women and a few young ones - as well as a child who was fidgeting all the time. The women seemed to be of the social status of maidservants - actual and potential - and called me didi (older sister - an address of respect) and used the honorific "you." But on the other hand, when I used the same honorific "you" to them, they were uncomfortable. One woman - an old one - said, "Why call us apni (vous/usted)? Call us tumi (tu)." We started talking. Initially they were uncomfortable, not used to nor trusting of social exchange with superiors. My clothes, accent, way of holding myself, my vocabulary all show my class as well, as an employer of women like themselves. A kid who was driving her mother and us insane provided something to talk about. But at the same time parts of the conversation were somewhat disturbing for me. "See this didi-moni," they said to her, "keep quiet or she'll get really mad at you." This of course had an efffect on the kid because she had accompanied her mother to the employer's house - where the ladies of the house, the powers that be - had told her to keep quiet, to sit still, or had probably even given her a candy sometimes. "How come you are here at this time?" I asked. "No cooking for the evening?" "Aunt here cooked in the afternoon while we were at work," said one of the younger women. "Nothing much to cook anyway. They can heat that up and eat later." "You are sisters?" I asked. The two young women sitting with the kid laugh - how could we be together if we were? How foolish of me - married women living together in a family were sisters-in-law of course! "So you like plays," I continued. "Well, we saw more palas (indigenous plays) when we lived in the village. I still see quite a few during the Puja season when I visit my father," said one of the young women, "but here in the city there is not much by the way of pala. Kids from the neighbourhood put on one in the field of the library during Saraswati Puja - but now what we see are movies in Aleya (nearby movie theatre)." "Hindi movies?" I asked. "Hindi and Bengali both." "Do you understand Hindi?" "Very little - but there are songs, dances and lots of fights - if you look at what they do you get it sort of." "Which do you like best?" "Hindi," said a couple of women. Of the old women who were silent so far, one said, "I saw a Bengali movie some years ago. It was a holy picture - about visiting some distant shrines in the Himalayas." She touched her folded palms to her forehead. "Didima does not like songs and dances," explained someone. "But you do?" "Well I do - but also I like Bengali films - more feelings, very sad - I saw one the other day and I cried a lot. I really liked it." At this moment they announced the play was beginning. "Please quieten down now," said the voice, "and mind your kids. Don't let them run around wildly or scream." At a distance I saw a friend, who heads the Democratic Women's Federation for this area, dragging two urchins by the arm.

The play was about different stages of revolutionary development - the story of a mother's love for her son slowly changing into an understanding of the revolutionary process. Firmly established within the frame of class struggle, Brecht traces a movement from the immediate and the local into class consciousness. The protagonists of the play are working class. The main protagonist is a woman, and there are quite a few women in the play. The world protrayed is that of the poor and the problems dealt with are the everyday worries of the working class - strikes, lay-offs, etc. In terms of content and concerns, there was quite a lot for the audience to identify with, including the beginning point of the transition, in which a mother gets involved with politics - not to be politically engaged but to protect her son - and agrees to take the risk of getting caught. She is an illiterate, god-fearing, unpoliticized working-class woman. Many of the women there could identify with this woman, at least more than I could. And yet the play seemed to happen even farther away than that - at a level which was not higher, but more abstract. It seemed distant, artificial; stiff, and yet sentimental. It had a kind of ideological blindness to everyday life that was all the more emphasized by the posters of Lenin, the slogans on placards or cloth banners, the red flag of the strikers, and the heroic stance of the dying worker. The play seemed like a garish, over-coloured political poster. The performance was both rigid and timid, as though the director did not know the terms of the play or the politics, but had copied the stances, sequences and groupings from a Soviet poster book. The image of the working class came from book to life, not the other way.

And of course this problem was heightened because not only was there an established convention of acting, but also the names of the characters, their clothes (not as important for men as for women), and their food were alien. But the most important distancing device was that of language. The workers, in the play as a whole, spoke in the language of "political literature," in the language of pamphlets and posters. And finally there was the stage - the raised proscenium stage - which in this field, where the audience was on the ground, made the action seem to happen at a literally "elevated" level and marked it off from "life." This was didactic theatre to educate the masses, to inspire them to class consciousness, to expose them to the different elements of revolutionary struggle, and to hold before them a typical example. It was a highly normative theatre.

What did it really tell the audience about class relations and organizations? How did it organize the relations during this performance, in this setting itself? How did it depict class and gender relations, for instance?

During the break and even during the performance I spoke to people. The director had great expectations of this production. The Party had approved of it - that is why they were invited here - and later in the year he was taking it to the industrial workers. So whether or not the "masses" related to this play was an important thing to find out.

My impression was that people were watching the play intently. This audience of three to four thousand people was very quiet. The women I sat with never talked, except to ask me at times what was being said (the microphone was not always working so well) or to quieten the kids. During the break I asked the young woman next to me how she liked it. She pondered a bit and then said, "I like it - I don't know - it's different from the palas we see at home. It's got less story - no kings or queens - it's not about the gods. In fact it's hardly got a story at all except that he (Pavel, the son) dies and she is sick and then she gets up to go out and gets into a fight with people - they hit her. I can't get what that's all about, the copper (Russia and World War I). To be honest I can't get this story, but I like some of it. I think they are kind of communist." "Why?" I asked. "What makes you say that?" "The flags," she said, "they have flags like that in front of the Party office in our neighbourhood." "Are there communists in your village?" I asked. "Many," she said. "The cultivators are turning communist." "Why is that?" "Because they help out the poor," she replied.

During this conversation the others were listening with a keen interest. Now I got offered a pan (betel leaf) from a little box tied at the sari end of one of the elderly women. The other young woman who was in a green sari and liked Hindi movies now spoke up. She said, "I knew they were communists from the very beginning - way before they brought the red flag. Remember they were speaking about strikes. I have seen a lot of strikes. When they closed the Usha Company and laid off workers, I worked at a house near there. Every morning I saw people at the gate - they spoke - god, so loudly! - like everyone around them was deaf! They kept on saying, "You have to accept our demands." "So did you like the play?" I asked. "The pieces I understood, but they were not speaking like we do. When people speak like that I don't understand. I get something of what's going on - the old woman had got into the strike somehow - and then some fights, but I don't get what happens. They want a biplab (revolution) - but there are all these words. For instance, what does 'bourgeois' mean?" I said, "Well, the rich - the malik (the owner) - rich businessmen." "Well, why don't they just say that?" An old woman said, "They were saying it's a play about mother - but where's the mother in this?" "There is a mother - you that woman in the blue dress?" replied another. "That's a mother! She's dressed in a frock like a little girl." "Grandmother," said one of the girls, "that mother is not like you and me. It's white people's mother."

*

These two descriptions speak for themselves, because they are not simply an expression of an immediate experience but, to quote Brecht, they each record an experience with "something equivalent to comment being incorporated in it." But there are a few points to which the reader's attention must be drawn, because these are basic issues of socialist/communist cultural practices, at the heart of revolutionary social transformation. Since socialism/communism matures in bourgeois society, we have to watch out for contradictions, both in terms of maintaining or smuggling in bourgeois social relations and cultural values, and in terms of overturning them. The contradictions operate mainly at two levels: a) using bourgeois dramatic forms and physical or social locations and bourgeois social relations to perform socialist/communist theatre; and b) at the level of agency, implicating the social relations between the classes which are represented and representing. It is obvious that those who are being represented by the middle class cannot take part in creating their own version of life or offer their own political analysis. Yet the overt political intention of the producers is socialist/communist, and within this political framework the lower classes are seen as the historical protagonists for class struggle and revolution.

Language and Liberation: A Study of Political Theatre in West Bengal

Thus we must detach the phenomena from the form in which they are immediately given and discover the intervening links which connect them to their core, their essence. In so doing, we shall arrive at an understanding of their apparent form and see it as the form in which the inner core necessarily appears. It is necessary because of the historical character of the facts, because they have grown in the soil of . . . society. This twofold character, the simultaneous recognition and transcendence of immediate appearance is precisely the dialectical nexus.

GEORGE LUKACS, *History & Class-consciousness*

In 1944 a theatre movement called the Indian People's Theatre Association was born. It was a novel phenomenon because it was organized on a national scale, it was noncommercial and, most importantly, an attempt to use culture for political mobilization and to raise consciousness about politics and society. Culture itself was seen as organizable and a site for class struggle rather than as a matter of individual creativity and spontaneity. Created under the auspices of the united Communist Party of India, carried forward by the massive participation of the urban intelligentsia, this movement largely shaped the course of modern Indian theatre. Today's "group theatre movements" or the progressive theatre all acknowledge its legacy. The birth was dramatic; in 1944 in a working-class district of Bombay, "the red capital of India," the IPTA held its inaugral conference and announced its motto with a great flourish: "The People's Theatre Stars the People."

With the arrival of this new protagonist, "the people," onto the theatrical stage the IPTA also announced a change in the Indian political scene. The same protagonist "the people" had also become the new revolutionary agent under the name of the proletariat as a combination of the urban working class and the landless and land-poor peasantry. The so-called "natural" leaders of the people - the landlords, the national bourgeoisie, and even the middle-class intelligentsia - had to yield place to this class at the theoretical level. Communist theories learnt from Marx, Lenin, and the Bolsheviks had no provision for any other revolutionary hero.

This new communist politics totally radicalized the theatre scene in undivided Bengal. The focus of theatre shifted from the commercial stage to the amateur political stage and for the first time since the inception of Bengali theatre in the 1860s peasants and workers walked the boards of the stage in nonmenial roles, as the organizers of their own struggles. Stages no longer reverberated with the heroic rantings and tragic declamations of the last kings and princes of India. In plays such as Bijan Bhattacharya's *The New Harvest* (*Nabanna*) or *The Confession* (*Jabanbandi*) a definite attempt was made to show the peasant's progress from powerlessness to power. From being portrayed as the victims of the 1943 famine they were transformed into the members of a peasant collective who promised a fair fight to their oppressors in the next round. This same spirit, sharpened through the struggles of the Telengana and the Bengal share-croppers (*Tebhaga Andolan*), found its expression in songs such as:

> Watch out, take care,
> Sharpen your scythes,
> Brothers, guard your rice and pride,
> For
> We will never again give up
> This rice
> That we have sowed with our blood.

(Telegana was a peasant movement (1948-51), involving two to three million people, organized mainly around demands for the redistribution of land.)

These were new songs and plays about new times and new politics. And they needed, and were couched in, a new language. The Bengali of the middle class - the gentlemen, the academics, and the literateurs - no longer sufficed; a different Bengali was resorted to - a Bengali spoken by the millions in the countryside, in the city slums. The middle-class activist in search of a language to expose exploitation and to give a voice to the new hero, "the people," turned to the "dialects" of different areas and the languages of the streets, the slums and different occupations.

Popular language became a matter of deep concern for the IPTA particularly as its mainstay were members of the urban intelligentsia who engaged in a representational and educative politics. After all, "the people's theatre" which "starred" the people did so with the help of those who were formally educated and Westernized, equally removed from the countryside and the city slums. What were presented as people's stories were in most cases neither created by the people nor narrated in their own voices. It was the middle-class playwrights, with sympathetic observations of the miseries of the people, who wrote the plays, and it was middle-class actors and actresses who put on tattered clothes, carried begging bowls or sticks and spears, and spoke in dialects carefully erasing the traces of the "proper" or "high" Bengali they had spoken all their lives. And yet given the time and the embryonic state of communist organization, the situation was unavoidable. Consequently the problem of the medium of communication assumed large proportions since the project of this new political theatre was to be easily understood by the people, to represent popular reality both to them and the middle class, and to legitimize popular-folk forms as culture. This project groped for a new aesthetic and voiced a demand for a "realist" theatre; outside and unaware of the European Marxist debate over "realism" the term was used to indicate the creation of an "authentic picture" of popular life and contemporary reality. Language was an indisputable element in this effort at "authenticity."

In conveying the popular reality this new theatre sought to bridge the gap between the rural and the urban worlds as well as that between the middle and working classes. It sought to convey to the middle class in particular some knowledge about how the subaltern classes lived and the severity of their day-to-day existence. The task of producing a realist art in this context often meant that of a faithful description of the surface of life rather than a dramatization of social analysis. As such the new theatre dismantled the palatial settings of the old stage and put up tin-can huts and torn burlap backdrops, replaced their tin swords with hammers and sickles, and filled the soundtracks with beggars' cries, the sounds of whiplashes and slogans rather than songs of courtesans. The dialogue naturally followed suit and the declamatory, rhetorical prose or blank verse were substituted with rural speech, street or factory talk, or even broken sentences. The result seems to have been particularly convincing to the middle class. The newspaper reviewers of *The New Harvest,* for example, and the established commercial actors, were all equally struck by the novelty and the lifelikeness of this new "beggars' opera." It was felt that the use of new types of language was the main graphic tool for bringing the people's reality into the middle-class world. The use of dialect in particular was the hallmark of authenticity of the "real" portrayal of the life of the "real" people of Bengal.

While this equation of realism with a "slice-of-life" approach to reality provided the middle class with a sense of the other kinds of lives lived by the poor, it left unanswered and unposed some major questions regarding analytical and explorative ways of uncovering the social relations that structured those lives. It also took "reality" for granted, blocked questions regarding the methods of this "realism" and equated a "real" portrayal with a naturalistic mode of depiction. It often diverted the cultural activists towards an empiricist rather than an analytical and historical-materialist approach. Preoccupied with an immediate event or an image, the playwrights often left no dramatic provision for the extra-local character of the social forces that informed them. *The New Harvest* (1944), for example, while providing a vivid portrayal of the sufferings of a famine-stricken, once well-to-do peasant household, gives us little or no indication of the social forces that structure and surround these lives. Nor is the devastation produced by the famine of 1943 (one and a half to three million are estimated to have died in it) made comprehensible by the presence of a few hoarders, black marketeers, and brothel keepers.

This uncontextualized famine assumes the character of natural cataclysm which a careful build-up of dialogue in dialect, capturing moments of suffering, rage, and despair, only enhances rather than historicizes. The concentration of the playwrights and the production (with special light effects, a revolving stage, and naturalist makeup and acting techniques) is too much on the surface, on the empirical immediate, which, of course, makes the last scene about collectivization and militancy seem empty and rhetorical. It lacks the dynamism of a social process and becomes iconic rather than political since organization cannot happen "in general" but must be context-specific. And yet this play, produced out of a real sympathy for the plight of the people, and unique in attempting to assign to the people an initiator's role, with all its shortcomings was seen by the middle class as the people's own version of the 1943 famine. When we ponder over the reasons for such a belief we can only come to the conclusion that it was due to the creation of a stereotypical environment of poverty and a dialogue in dialect. The attention of the audience was also riveted to the high display of feelings, which could be recognized by the middle-class audience as being noble enough or "pathetic" enough to be worth heightening. The naturalism of language completes the illusion of reality. A lifelike copy seemed to be the aim of the producers, and the audience responded to this by finding in the play the "real thing." But because questions regarding the social construction of reality, or the mode called "realism," were yet to be asked it remained unnoticed that often what passed for the peasants' reality was the middle-class version of the rural world. These plays fulfilled certain norms or expectations of the middle-class audience, which is why perhaps the reviewers could talk about the lead actor as being "more of a peasant than a peasant could be." Through the naturalism of acting and language the issue shifted from politics not only to imitation, but often also to the imitation of an idealized or stereotypical version of popular reality.

While such idealization came from the communist movement and its overall social impact, the stereotypes of class, gender, age, good and evil mostly came from the conventions of the bourgeois commercial stage and petty-bourgeois or middle-class social ethos. Large numbers of the audience and most of the cultural producers were brought up within these theatrical conventions and this ethos. The theatrical conventions had naturalized certain stereotypical forms of characterization and emotions. Neither was the influence of the English stage and dramatic tradition negligible in the development of these stage conventions. Overall they encoded the morality and the world view of a semifeudal semibourgeois urban population, not that of the working class or the peasantry. This largely unconscious legacy of what was once "the theatre," in conjunction with an imitative realism, generated a form and a content which exposed the new theatre to the danger of subordinating the culture and politics of the very people they wished to help or idealized by offering a decontextualized, embourgeoisified version of their story. Again we may look at Bhattacharya's *The New Harvest* for an example. Here, in the character of the old peasant "patriarch" Pradhan, Shakespeare's King Lear receives his peasant incarnation. Put through the trials of famine, fire, and flood he rises to great sonorous declamations of rage and despair. His pathos and all that he declaims provide the audience more with echoes of Shakespeare than the voice of the Bengali peasantry. That it is in a dialect does not change this, though the dialect lends a touch of the authenticity of peasant life or character. Other examples of conventionalization and non-popular ethics and world view may be found in the portrayals of women and children: quaint scenes of domesticity and moments of pathos introduced through dying, lisping, precocious babes and frequent weeping. The repudiation of these conventions does not signify that the peasantry or the slum-dwellers have no personal lives, no hearts and minds; but rather indicates what moments of their lives are selected to be put on view, or what is projected into their lives by the middle class, and to what extent these are in tune with the middle class's experience and conception of theatre and morality. It would often seem that with other clothes, other settings, and in another language for dialogue, many of these scenes could fit into the genre of drawing-room comedies. It also seems as though the middle-class progressives measured the "humanity" of the poor in terms of their approximation to middle-class morality and emotional life. The idea seems to have been to point out how much like "us" they were; that they too laughed, cried, loved, and lamented like "us." Without disputing a genuine claim for an emotional life for the subaltern classes one could ask the question - "But do they laugh, cry, sigh, and lament about the same things or love or die in the same way?" And if they did not, would they be any less "human"? Must not one avoid the values and practices of the middle class becoming universalized into the human practice? Is the creation of the "other" simply a matter of likeness and imitation - sounding something like the other? Dialect, occupational languages, broken sentences, stage props, lighting, and naturalistic acting may all contrive to lull our minds while satisfying our eyes and ears.

The minds of the colonial middle-class audiences can also be lulled, for instance by the echoes of Shakespeare, by allusions to a knowledge of "tragic" conventions; the echoes may divert the audience from the fact that this is not a mythic, structural use of Shakespeare but a reduction of a dramatic text to a story, a set of typical speeches and fixed theatrical devices. The plays of Aeschylus or Sophocles, or of Shakespeare for that matter, have been often reworked or re-elaborated as myths rather than as stories told through historically specific stage conventions. Sartre in *The Flies,* Brecht in the retelling of *Timon of Athens,* Aime Cesaire in *The Tempest,* Athol Fugard in *The Island,* to name a few playwrights, have reworked certain basic themes to represent Nazism, capitalism, imperialism, and apartheid respectively. But in *The New Harvest* the thematic inner core, the mythic element of *King Lear,* has been bypassed in favour of a ranting, pathetic emotionalism. The aim here seems to be a piece that rouses the audience's emotions, not a comprehensible presentation of the peasant's world.

II

The tradition of IPTA continues in the cities of India. The Group Theatre Movement of Calcutta works within this tradition and abounds with plays about the Bengali peasantry. As before, fewer plays are written or performed about the urban working class, the slum or pavement dwellers than about the peasantry. And in all this the same kind of problem that faced the IPTA nearly forty years ago continues to haunt the world of theatre. Since the 1940s the urban progressive or left-wing culture milieu is that of middle-class performers and writers trying to enlighten their own class, exposing horror stories from the countryside or the slums. The practice of an imitative realism also continues in all good faith and political intention. Plays abound with attempts to reproduce an immaculate surface of life which comes into direct conflict within the play with a kind of "iconic realism," which presents us with the peasant or the woman of the people, the worker, etc. This characterization is not so much a Lukacsian "type," a representative class character as he actually exists in the present conjuncture of social relations in Bengal, but more a set of fixed, static, idealized images of who he should be, given an abstract formulation of revolutions. As imitative realism suffers from an empiricist approach so this icon-building of workers and peasants suffers from an idealism and a political prescriptiveness. In this, revolution is not seen as a developing social process produced by certain historical classes beginning from where they are, but as an event which could be approximated by only the perfect character types. Even though this idealization came about as a result of a change in the political perspective it moved away from the ground of history, took on an ideological character, and complemented the empirical fixity of naturalist description. Since here as well a process-oriented view of society and revolution was lacking, and yet a revolution or resistance was integral to the plot, these iconic representations accomplished this as a part of the idealization itself. They are revolutionary because they are who they are, not because of, and in the way of, who they can become. They "embody" class-consciousness rather than "become" class conscious, much in the manner in which icons embody holiness. Hence they accomplish the task of resistance as indeed they must since in terms of the narrative development the play begins from the last victorious scene.

The use of dialect or appropriate language, however, lends these iconic idealizations the touch of typicality, and often, as for instance in Utpal Dutt's play *Titu Mir*, serves as a substitute for class analysis. In this play the peasant hero Titu Mir (the term "peasant" here includes rich farmers such as Titu) stages an idealized uprising against the foreign invaders and dies a martyr's death. The historical Titu Mir as a member of a landed class, the social relations of contemporary Bengal, and the colonialist penetration are nowhere to be found, but instead we have a play in universalist terms outside of the frame of "mere" history. Titu Mir and his followers as well as the foreign invaders are inflated beyond lifesize. One set was born to make heroic sacrifices and the other to dominate; they embody the primal forces of good and evil. As is common with this kind of play, exploitation or domination remains utterly nonspecified or undifferentiated, making it impossible to grasp the real political process. There is about as much real political dynamism in this play as quickly shuffling through a pack of heroic pictures! It is basicaly a series of static images gaining momentum through a successive placement. Here the role of language is not only important in masking an ideological approach to politics, but also in distancing it into patriotism. This play, because it is placed in a distant past, has less of a clash between mimetic and iconic types of realism.

But outside of the naturalist use of language and the political rhetoric of the prescriptive ideological mode there has also developed a use of language that displays and clarifies the social relations of domination. Instead of a sustained use of a dialect which has a greater chance of presenting a middle-class version of reality than that of the working class or the peasantry, the playwrights often combine different types of speech to encode the different class views and relations. This method, instead of drawing the audience into an illusion of reality, distances the viewer and facilitates a clearer observation and a critical perspective. On the one hand, the typicality of the speech with its particular use of idioms, images, and constructions gives a sense of the group in itself, its cohesive community consciousness; on the other hand, the presence of other types of speech makes of language an area of class struggle as well. A good example of this is the use of language in a play by Arun Mukherji called *The Tale of Marich* (*Marich-samvad*). Here Marx's statement about history as being the history of class struggles is dramatized over a long span of time. The narrative time ranges from the epic days of the *Ramayana* to the present, moving from the legendary world of the man-god Rama and the demon king Ravana of Srilanka to the streets of contemporary Calcutta. In between Mukherji provides a detour through the United States of America. At each phase he presents an individual's response to the pressures exerted by the state and the ideological hegemony of the ruling classes, until he reaches the possibility of class struggle through an individual's growing class-conscious response. In each phase the play emphasizes the particularity of the situation while containing it within an overall framework of domination and response. In this way, each scene which would have been impossible out of its own historical setting is also dovetailed into the next one. Much of this dialectical complexity is realized through the use of different types of speech.

The play starts in a Calcutta street where a street entertainer - a juggler/magician/singer/player - is drumming up his audience with a high sales pitch. Like all conmen he promises the impossible. He claims to be able to resurrect the mythic figures of the *Ramayana,* but also, in attempting to please other tastes, he promises scenes that appeal to modern sensibilities. He promises scenes from America as well as from the low life of Bengal. The play moves through a hilarious mixture of these levels creating confusions and mix-ups, but also using these confusions to achieve a clarity and continuity. The confusion created by the frequent mistakes made by the ruling classes about their different parts (sliding mid speech from the dialogue of the mythic tyrant Ravana to that of the state department or CIA official) also serves as a basis for political clarity. Similarities and dissimilarities in the historical particularities build towards a resolution where all the subordinated characters get out of the magician-dramatist's directorial control and refuse to die in the service of or at the hands of the ruling classes. The shift in the use of speech indicates alteration without the use of curtains, changes of scenes, or situations. The epic characters (who frequently feature in the popular theatrical form known as jatra) speak in a highly declamatory blank verse with which the audience is familiar from its experience at the jatras and the other Bengali plays. The exhortation by the demon king Ravana to Marich, the turncoat pacifist demon who is pining away for Rama the man-god, well known to all Bengalis from the *Ramayana,* now takes on the tone of political harangue by the Congress (nationalist) leaders as they preach patriotism to the poor. This is further emphasized by the litany of patriotism delivered by a priest figure in mock-Sanskrit (Bengali spoken with Sanskrit endings). The contemporary relevance of this scene is further emphasized as the actor in Ravana's part confuses his cue and immediately descends to dialect. Now transformed into the landlord's bailiff he browbeats the ex-retainer of the landlord, a landless peasant called Isvar, to break a few heads during the rent collection. For both Marich and Isvar individual indebtedness, gratefulness to a good patron, patriotism, or the good of the village (identified with the good of the landlord) are used to prod them to identify with their oppressors.

The scope extends even further, laterally to the United States, rather than into the past, where a lackey of the state department harasses a liberal upper-middle-class young man to go to Vietnam to fight for his president and his country. As the patriotic injunction of President Kennedy booms through the auditorium - "Ask not what your country can do for you but what you can do for your country" - the reply comes from the young man Gregory in a monotonous, dead Bengali of the right-wing daily newspaper *Ananda Bazar Patrika.* More of the same is continued by the state department official. This is strongly contrasted by the peasant speech of Isvar and the half-gentrified dialect of the bailiff, whose speech betrays class origin and present political affiliations. The audience is further entertained by the lumpenized street Bengali of the magician. The issue of understanding reality is no longer posed in terms of imitation, or lifelikeness, but of an overall dynamic version of the social relations that structure domination of different kinds. This particular use of language as integral to the narrative breaks the bourgeois dichotomy between form and context. There is no attempt here to present the poor peasant's world or worldview by trying to step into his shoes through an act of empathy, but instead to display the relations of inequality that entangle the different classes. There is a clear shift here from aiming at portraying the authentic peasant experience (which the middle class is structurally, existentially barred from doing) to politicizing a problem no matter where it is located.

Other than using language politically in some plays, Bengali theatre has a remarkable instance of dramatization of the issue of the politics of language. *The Tin Sword* (*Tiner Talwar*) by Utpal Dutt is a play about the necessity of a new aesthetic. It includes in its purview the problem of language as a medium of representation and communication, not only with middle-class audiences but with the people themselves. The first scene centres on the encounter between Benimadhab Chatujye (a drunk director of a commercial theatre) and a street sweeper who is also a latrine cleaner. The drunk Benimadhab is accosted by this character from the lower depths, who sticks out his head from a manhole and throws some dirt at the brahmin to affront him and attract his attention. Benimadhab, however, takes no offence at this, and instead gets into a conversation with him, trying to convince the sweeper to visit the theatre. At this point the following interchange takes place:

Beni: . . . so you don't go to plays?

Sweeper: Why should I? What's in it for the likes of us anyway? The babus (gentlemen) will live it up at the theatres, screw around with women from the market, and use language that we can't understand. (*Pours out some more dirt.*) Better to watch the dancing girls or ramlila in our slum. This peacock Mayur play or whatever that you mentioned - what's that about?

Beni: Mayurbahan, you see, is the prince of Kashmir. The story . . .

Sweeper: Damn the prince! Why do you have to do this? Get all dressed up in your red and blue clothes and tinsels, paint your faces and play at kings and princes? After all this education why must you tie a tin sword around your waist and act childish?

Beni: Tin sword? Childish?

Sweeper: Why can't you dress as who you are? Can't you see that there is a lot of dirt on you?

Acknowledging that "there's a lot of dirt" on the middle class as a party to class exploitation, Utpal Dutt attempted to transform this tin sword of theatre, a plaything of the middle class and the entrepreneur, into a real sword, a revolutionary weapon. The use of language in this play is astounding in grasping the complexity that structures the sociocultural reality of a colonized middle class. He captures some of the existing contradictions in terms of dialect vs "high" Bengali, colloquial vs formal Bengali, occupational language of the street vs academic Bengali, and finally in terms of English used by the educated "Young Bengal" confronted by the anticolonial Bengali of the national liberation movement. The issue of realism has moved very far away from its first groping phase.

In problematizing some of the "givens" of the earlier IPTA organizers the group theatre movement has moved a step ahead. But this has been possible because the IPTA has had a real impact on Indian theatre, and, however unsatisfactorily, has made the demand for a new realist aesthetic. It is not surprising that this most conscious, unique play about language, reality, and politics - *The Tin Sword* - comes from a playwright, actor, and director whose beginnings lie in the IPTA. He and others have often considered it a political problem that the middle class often stood in for the people. Even as long ago as the thirties the Bengali poet Jatindranath Sengupta remarked in a satirical poem on the populism of the middle class:

Remember, brothers,
We are not peasants,
We are the peasants' barristers.

This substitution was and remains as problematic as if Harriet Beecher-Stowe or some other white American writer (no matter how sympathetic) were to write about the "authentic" black experience, or their Uncle Toms or Elizas were to be seen as "types" of the black American, or all black people were to be presented as undifferentiated, stereotypical characters. When the oppressed fight against using the oppressor's language and establish the legitimacy of their own speech, the politics this process involves is radically different from the one where members of the oppressing classes use the oppressed's language to sympathetically mimic them into respectability. At that point even idealization does not compensate for the harm done through the process. Not only are we in danger of an illusion or a standing-in effect, but also the politics this implies is, at its best, not brought beyond the immediate level of depiction of misery. With a middle-class audience it might have some effect of sensitization to poverty, though mainly of evoking an empty emotionalism; should there actually be a popular audience, it would merely replay for them what they already know. Both the slice-of-life approach and making an icon of a peasant or a working-class hero seem singularly devoid of organizational implications. A great deal more can be done by the progressive left-wing theatre activists by placing themselves (in class terms) and their language into the plays. This may liberate the political forces of theatre itself and lift it from an empiricism and idealism, from liberal guilt or politics of sympathy into a real politics of class struggle. Then with or without the use of dialect we might still attain a realism.

Representation and Class Politics in the Theatre of Utpal Dutt

The Context and Scope of Utpal Dutt's Theatre

For time flows on, and if it did not it would be a poor lookout for those who have no golden tables to sit at. Methods wear out, stimuli fail. New Problems loom up and demand new techniques. Reality alters; to represent it the means of representation must alter too.

BERTOLT BRECHT, *The Popular and the Realistic*

When theatre becomes a matter of conscious political intervention, rather than a spontaneous expression of politics and class, complexities around the question of representation become crucial. Theatre now has to move beyond the level of an aesthetic and coherent construct, to being accountable and explanatory (not only expressive) of the reality which requires intervention. This speaks of a politicization, of ways of knowing and seeing, as well as of depicting. This argues for a transperancy between methodological and representational terms of realism and socialism. Their enterprises become interchangeable, and we note that the problem of realism, of defining reality and depicting or describing it is not unique to artists but one that all socialist/communist activists share in common. It is only to the extent that they can analyze and work with the existing social relations and organizations, that they are successful in making a meaningful intervention. Marx and Engels for instance speak of a socialism as being utopian or scientific, truly socialist rather than merely political (i.e. bourgeois), depending on the socially grounded nature of the political analysis and their forms of organization. In the case of artistic-cultural intervention, however, the problem of realism and representation is further complicated by the particular and complex nature of the productive mediations. The class character and the political adequacy of a play is not only expressed by the analytical or ideological intention of the playwright or director but the actual politics that can only be arrived at from the concrete work itself. The stated theoretical or ideological position may surround and abet it, but it is the actual play, or the theatre project as a whole, which will uncover the actual class character and politics of the project. Thus the study of any political theatre must attend to the formal representational or mediational apparatus of the theatre along with the stated or suggested epistemological, methodological and ideological standpoints. In light of the political importance of aesthetic realism the intention of this paper is to examine the realization process of an actual theatrical project of a very important member of the present-day political theatre in West Bengal, namely Utpal Dutt. But before doing that let us briefly review the period that connects him to the Indian Peoples Theatre Association's last national convention.

Let us begin with a brief reminder about the political project of the Indian Peoples Theatre Association (IPTA). A look at IPTA's history shows how as the contradictions inherent in the liberal nationalist independence of India became apparent after 1947, the accumulated contradictions within the communist movement intensified as well. The divergent political tendencies, cultural perspectives and practices that were suspended in the loose framework of "progressivism" due to the necessity of a united front in the context of national independence, no longer held. The CPI and its cultural outreach the IPTA fragmented around the same time riven by intricately related and similar problems. 1956 was the year of the last national convention of IPTA, and the CPI split into two in 1964. In the summer of 1979 emerged The Group Theatre Federation. The reasons for forming the Federation were put forward by Jacchan Dastidar, the secretary of the organization since 1979, in the journal *Theatre Bulletin*. According to Dastidar:

> For many long decades the group theatres were fulfilling their social responsibilities through their theatre productions. Increasingly economic pressures in the country, continuous increase in the rental of stages, increase in the price of advertisements in local daily newspapers, the increase in the price of miscellaneous objects and facilities necessary for theatre production, all forced the theatre groups to go through an unbearable existence. But even so these theatre groups, in their isolation, carried on their individual initiatives. This is the situation which forced them to realize that perhaps they would not be able to exist for too long in this way. "The Group Theatre Federation" is a result of this realization. (*Theatre Bulletin*, 1980, p. 9)

Easily comparable to the IPTA manifesto in its catholicity of taste and politics, the manifesto of the Group Theatre Federation is another attempt at forming a common platform for "progressive" playwrights. The Federation has a place for all theatre groups which are noncommercial or amateur, except those which, according to the manifesto, are busy

> trying to keep alive life-denying customs and superstitions, trying to stimulate lust and sensuality, attempting to vindicate self-centred and fascistic fantasies, or propagandizing for the maintenance of the status quo of the present society, which is contaminated by religious blindness, bigotry, racism and communalism, as well as those who not only reject the demand for decent human existence but actively oppose it through their art - except for those groups - all others can become members of this Federation. (*Theatre Bulletin,* 1980, p. 9)

One other similarity exists between this progressive and humanist attempt and IPTA's, which is that also in the case of the Federation the founding inspiration came from a communist party. The encouragement and initiative came from the CPI(M)'s cultural policy, its activist front, and this has important implications for theatre groups in West Bengal, since the Left Front government of West Bengal has a CPI(M) leadership. This connection with the state and the governing party has been both an added attraction for joining the Federation, as well as cause for criticism of the government for practising favouritism. But the Federation, which openly acknowledges this relationship to the state, does not apologize for it and points out the active attempts by the Left Front Government to patronize cultural activities. *Theatre Bulletin* published a statement to this effect:

> It is the same Left Front Government which has formed, for the first time [in West Bengal], an advisory committee which holds a leadership position among the theatre groups. What they [the Left Front] have already achieved, or may achieve in the future, will be witnessed by the common people of the province. But at least the Left Front is thinking about groups like us. They recognize our contribution. Until now it was after all a non-left wing government which was in charge of the state of West Bengal, but they never thought about us or ever felt the necessity of even talking with us. (*Theatre Bulletin,* 1980, p. 10)

But in spite of frequent accusations by the non- or anti-CPI(M) participants of favouritism regarding funding or the manipulating of the cultural scene of West Bengal by the CPI(M) government, it becomes apparent from the advertisements in the theatre magazines, newspapers, different publications and the continuous proliferation of theatre groups in all corners of Calcutta, that there is no real cultural commissariat being maintained by the state or the Party. What there is, is an attempt to promote a theatre ideology from an established communist perspective which has a longstanding history in Bengal/India. This general ambience pervades a huge amount of theatre produced by groups which are not CPI(M)-affiliated and even anti-CPI(M).

In this broad theatre spectrum interests range from a directly political theatre of class struggle to ones of populism, civil liberties, and formal experimentalism. New streams of theatre philosophies and forms were and are feeding into this area. Along with the old IPTA tradition of socialist realism and revolutionary romanticism learnt from the USSR, there has developed a cumulative history of fascination with old classics such as Ibsen and Chekov, existentialism and the theatre of the absurd - of both Sartre and Beckett - with the neorealism of Pinter, Pirandello's symbolist theatre, along with the "epic" and "total" theatre of Brecht and Piscator. These provided, and still do, the main resources for adaptation and translation. There is also an interest in jatra, hitherto missing from the Bengal IPTA, though in its theatrized, urbanized, and commercial form. Different "folk" conventions have also minimally influenced the new political theatre. The breakup of IPTA, then, did not put an end to a development of Bengal's progressive theatre but its different tendencies began to develop relatively separately from each other.

In spite of the breakup of IPTA and the CPI, some things continue to be the same. Not only do the cultural and political producers come from the same class background, but the general predisposition to Europeanization that was put in place in the nineteenth century, and supplied a vital ingredient of the subjective consciousness of the middle class throughout the colonial period continues as well. The theatrical traditions, that is, the representational options, also continued to be the same, with some additions from the post-Second World War era of Europe and the United States. Bourgeois cultural and theatre theories and practices, Bengali and Western (from the nineteenth century onwards), whose presence we detected in IPTA, still remain attractive and influential. The importance of older socialist/communist theatres of Europe and the Soviet Union is not diminished either as a result of the search for a proper typologically "communist" theatre. Socialist realism still continues to be influential, particularly among those who aim towards a direct theatre of class struggle under the auspices of any of the communist parties and can assume the name of Gananatya or people's theatre.

In this effervescence of theatre activities among the Bengali middle classes of Calcutta (reminiscent in scope, intensity, and splits of the last half of the nineteenth century), it is possible to discern four political tendencies. It must also be remembered however that they overlap and that there is a degree of nebulousness about them, since the boundaries between the formal or even the ideological conventions are by no means established. Roughly they could be characterized as follows:

a) A "progressive" theatre - interested in specific issues, for example, the social situation of women, from a "humanist" standpoint. Playwrights of this type are not directly or primarily interested in class or revolution. They see theatre as "art" rather than a site of or tool for politics.

b)A theatre of class - where there is an explicit interest in promoting proletarian revolution and class struggle. This may involve current international, national or local politics, and a willingness to work cooperatively with any of the organized communist parties, i.e. CPI, CPI(M), and CPI(ML). There is also an attempt to context the theatre to classical revolutionary theories of Marx, Engels, Lenin, Stalin and Mao.

c) A theatre with an exploratory interest in class and class struggle, rather than in the moment of revolution. It is not directly associated with party politics in West Bengal/ India, nor directly or canonically with the works of major communist thinkers, but is sensitized by the existence of communist parties, movements and a general body of literature on class and class struggle.

d) A utopian theatre of "humanism" where themes of alienation (psychological) and domination take the place of themes of class. Relying on spontaneity and moral change (change of heart), this theatre concentrates its attack on technology, consumption and money without a concept of class or capital and advocates a return to the "village society" and assumes the possibility of a resurrection of the pristine social and mental state. It displays a partial affinity for Gandhian philosophy.

Among these many tendencies our interest lies in exploring the works of Utpal Dutt, whom we place in the tradition of the second type of (directly political) theatre of revolutionary (proletarian) class struggle. Our particular emphasis is on his attempts to create a theory and practice of an epic-mythic project, a project that he sees as the goal of his theatre work. This exploratory exercise concentrates on how he, in the many roles of playwright, director, actor and critic, negotiates the different representational options in Bengali theatre through IPTA and after. His attempts are explored in terms of class consciousness and representational politics of Bengali communism. Our purpose is to take up the themes of representation and class struggle and to bare the class character of Utpal's theatre projects. From the "realism" of his formal apparatus and the class implications of his cultural theories we will come to some conclusions regarding the class character of a specific theatre project and of political theatre in West Bengal. This will also entail an examination of this playwright-director's use of local and foreign theatre traditions and cultural theories as well as an examination of their epistemological and ideological underpinnings.

Utpal Dutt

I came to the conclusion that in a colonial country a pure intellectual is a pure coward.
UTPAL DUTT, *Towards a Revolutionary Theatre*

Utpal Dutt as he stands now with his People's Little Theatre Group is the largest figure on the Bengali stage - political or otherwise. His work, as in the case of all other theatre producers, is whollly in Bengali. Yet it was not always so. Utpal Dutt's theatre trajectory is that of all of India's middle-class liberal, Westernized intellectuals. It moves from colonialism to nationalism, from English to Bengali, from Europe to India, and in a manner of speaking from liberalism to communism. This transformation is a matter of the development of a conscious political choice - often remaining within bourgeois nationalism with a tangential movement towards an anti-imperialism with clearly nationalist traces.

During the mid forties, Utpal Dutt was a student in St Xavier's, a Jesuit-administered English-medium college. There he became involved in theatrical production through a professor, Father Weaver, who was once in the Irish Abbey Theatre. Utpal learnt Shakespeare from him. It was not Father Weaver, however, but rather Geoffrey Kendal, who while touring India with the Old Vic company (1947-53) gave him his basic training and theatre canon, which was centred around Shakespeare. Whether as a young man learning the craft of bourgeois English theatre from Geoffrey Kendal, Utpal Dutt ever fantasized about becoming an "artist" and the universal nature of art and theatre, is not known to us. But by all accounts, he did not walk the boards for long before he decided on the political immediacy of theatre. According to him,

> In 1948 the communist party became illegal. Arrests, torture and gangsterism went on recklessly, and the complacent (secure) pursuit of theatre by the Little Theatre Group progressively began to seem ridiculous - a pointless hypocrisy. In June of 1948 we published a strong political tract in the programme notes of Romeo and Juliet. The article began with Gorky's letter to Stanislavsky and

> ended in a protest against the choking into silence of the voice of the IPTA. We also added such information in our article as recently devastated German fascism also began its march by attacking theatre. And later it is this article that kept on mocking us all the time. Miriam Stark was the lead actress of our group in those days - Rebecca of the film Michael. That forthright, straight-speaking woman said: "If we really believe in what we have written, then why are we acting in one classic after another, and for whom?" (Dutt, 1977, pp. 52-53)

As a result there was a production of *Julius Caesar* in modern costume:

> By modern we mean in the regalia of Italian fascism . . . without changing a single word Shakespeare's play became a highly contemporary play. I was able to see a dictator in Caesar who towered above his time and nation. When our Caesar (Ellis Abraham) got up to give his speech in a felt hat, and the senators in red and black greeted him with a resounding "heil," when the democratic Brutus (I) began to vacillate, faced with the inevitable bloodshed, when the extremist Cassius (Pratap) explained with his infallible logic the necessity of a bloody clash, and the cruel, conniving and cunning Anthony like any great fascist orator, mislead the masses, the play became a vast mirror of the contemporary world. (Dutt, 1977, p. 52)

This, even before he discovered that he could write plays, is the beginning of Utpal's life as a participant in political theatre. It was a response not to any abstract ideas of politics - but to the dark times of Indian independence, which was born in communal massacres, exodus, homelessness, partition of the country and communist repression. Utpal Dutt himself describes the response and the time for us.

> Anger thrashed around the rib cage in impotent frustration at the news of shooting of the political prisoners [of the CPI and of the Tebhaga movement], women murdered in Kakdwip, the earth reddened in Nayanpur, police firing in the IPTA performance at Dibrugar, reckless firing in the maidan and Hazra Park, firing on women's demonstration in Bow Bazar - and why is Little Theatre silent? (Dutt, 1977, p. 53)

From 1953 Utpal abandoned the practices of putting on plays in English, since the question of who the audience was became a crucial one. No matter how political a play may be - the very fact that it is in English, he felt, kills the politics of the play, since it must be played to an audience which is upper class and generally right wing. Utpal therefore looked to Bengali and European classics and sought out primarily a Bengali-speaking audience: Michael Madhusudan Dutt to Rabindranath Tagore from Bengal, and Shakespeare, Gorky, Brecht, Gogol, etc. "progressive" classics of all sorts translated and adapted from abroad, provided him with "progressive material" for building a theatre for raising popular consciousness.

His interest in classics was matched by his interest in a topical theatre for immediate consumption, namely "propaganda and agitation." He formly believed that these two types of theatre, i.e., classics and propaganda, are reconcilable in a fuller political theatre aesthetics. His involvement with propaganda and agitprop started in 1950. Invited to perform for IPTA in 1950, he joined the organization for ten months at the Central Calcutta branch and came under the influence of Panu Pal, a committed IPTA activist, who was then mounting a street play, *Chargesheet,* for the release of communist prisoners from the jails of independent India. Utpal sees this period as that of his political education both for theatre and for the election of 1952, which the CPI was allowed to participate in. Utpal's interest in the propaganda form continued beyond this period, through the rest of his life.

> I have written and played two dozen such plays [propaganda], even developing them to full 3 hour performances, and have revelled in them as an artist, not only as a political being. Critics there are who have contemptuously spurned these efforts as rude political propaganda and have written extensively on my naivete. I do not think that theatre can accomodate a thoroughly cynical, exhausted, mental octogenarian. (Utpal Dutt, 1982, p. 34)

Informational and analytical of political issues at hand, these plays bare the oppression of the Indian people, and attempt direct their political choice towards the different communist parties, particularly the CPI(M) since the 1970s. Utpal Dutt has also responded outside of the agit-prop framework to the intensive repression by the Indian state against progressive and communist activists, particularly in the state of West Bengal. Since 1967, that is, the beginning of the United Front electoral victory, and the rise of a Maoist movement (Naxalite), West Bengal experienced much terror from the state and its ruling party, Congress (M). These brutalities culminated in the Emergency of 1975-76. These are the times which are described, analyzed and responded to by plays such as *Barricade, Ebar Rajar Pala* (Enter the King), *Rifle, Dushapner Nagari* (Nightmare City), among others.

It is certainly the legacy of IPTA which enabled Utpal to connect the work of fundamental social transformation and involvement with communist politics, with that of theatre. The short agit-prop plays constitute an immediate, practical and political theatre. They are connected to a specific communist party's strategies and tactics, and respond to the contemporary Indian and international political scenes. Here much of the attention is directed to informing and educating both in terms of facts and taking a stand a part in organized party politics. An aesthetics of political immediacy justifies both the form and the content of this theatre - it is the aesthetics of propaganda agitation and direct activism.

But along with this practical and pragmatic approach, there is a broader political project in Utpal Dutt's theatre. It is in no sense propagandist, but an epistemological one, aimed towards reorienting the audience to the enduring, even "universal truth" about history, in terms of class struggle, class consciousness and national identity. This is the level with its own aesthetic of representation, which Rustam Bharucha misses, when like many other anti-communist critics he is driven into saying that Dutt "harangues his audience, and hypnotizes them with slogans, rhetoric, and spectacular stage devices" (Bharucha, p. xiii). This assessment is shallow, and involves a knee-jerk response to an activist theatre of the organized left and is applicable only, if at all, to the practical aspect of Utpal's theatre rather than to his larger project of the creation of politically philosophical revolutionary theatre. It is in relation to this larger historic/epic-mythic project, we will see, that Utpal Dutt rejects the very slogan-mongering and formula politics and propaganda theatre to which Bharucha reduces his work. Bharucha, had he known Bengali well, and read the full opus of Dutt's theatre criticism in Bengali, might have found ideas and sentiments that are surprisingly contradictory to those he attributes to Dutt. In a book called *Japenda Japan Ja* (Meditations and Pursuasions of Brother Japan), a dialogical, dramatic discussion on theatre and culture he ridiculed the formulaic political theatre of IPTA tradition. As he puts it,

> The architect of the new world Mao-tse-tung tried hard to humanize bulls like you. In his Yenan speech he said "get the content of your theatre from the present day struggles, but while writing use the examples of the ancient classics." What does that mean? It doesn't mean that you'll put an English character and a Bengali peasant on stage and show them fighting. What do your plays have in them? First a white man or landlord takes a whip and beats the daylight out of a bunch of peasants. They get a sight of heaven, fall down, scream, groan - "once we had

> rice in every home and now the landlord's taken it all." Then comes the communist - the vessel of all virtues, a good boy, who has done all his homework. He neither has any doubt, nor weakness, nor conflicts. Such a saint comes along and raises the consciousness of he peasants - they, having seen the light, go and beat up the landlord - curtain. Here endeth the theatre of people's theatre association. This is your formula. (Dutt, 1984, pp. 13-14)

Though this is not to say that Utpal Dutt does not use just this very formula, if it serves his immediate purpose, it indicates his full awareness of its limitations. He has a much more ambitious political theatre in mind.

This larger and more ambitious project is an epic project regarding history. It involves the creation of revolutionary myths through an epic mode. This is the central focus of our discussion in characterizing the politics of his theatre. The following lines give us a sense of how he envisions his work in this direction:

> From the very beginning of my theatre work we have tried to put revolution in a historical perspective. Studying social phenomena in isolation, assuming each phase of development as a whole, that is, substituting the general with the particular, is a universal bourgeois vice, which has infected "progressive" thinking as well. (Dutt, 1982, p. 28)

Historical amnesia, according to Utpal, created by the ideological hegemony of the local and foreign classes, has deprived the Bengali/Indian people of their historical, political and cultural identity. The work of political theatre is "to spread hatred, to preach hatred, to harp on hatred endlessly . . . for the imperialist, the capitalist, for the primeval beast called the feudal lord" (Dutt, 1982, p. 56). In order to do this we must re-learn our history. The truth about history is simple for him - of militant class and anticolonioal struggles. According to Utpal, to counter the propaganda of peace, which is actually an insiduous Gandhian politics of hate, political theatre must "expose the mendacious theories of peace as a trick of the ruling classes to dope the masses with masses of opium" (Dutt, 1982, p. 56). "Our task" is to fight this great historical lie and to point out that class rule in India has masqueraded in the Gandhian era with a face of peace and forgiveness.

This has mislead the people of India:

> We have been sickened no end by endless nonsense about peace and forgiveness . . . about Gandhi and the so-called Indian tradition of peace . . . But history tells us that India has staged some of the biggest genocides the world has ever seen. (Dutt, 1982, p. 56)

The masked violence of the ruling class must be countered by the open revolutionary violence of the people - and for this they must know the path travelled by others before them. The work of Utpal Dutt and the People's Little Theatre then is:

> to re-affirm the violent history of India, to re-affirm the martial tradition of its people, to re-count again and again the heroic tales of grand rebels and martyrs. (Dutt, 1982, p. 56)

Utpal Dutt proceeds to fulfill his task by recounting "moments" of confrontation between two opposing political forces. In this way he hopes to crystalize the class truths of history through what he calls "myths." The "myths" both embody and reveal the basic historical law, i.e., the law of class struggle, embedded in the historical events. They are what he calls "myths of revolution," or myths of "violence." They are heroic moments of national and international armed resistance. To these are added myths of national culture and culture heroes.

The historic mythic project of Utpal can be classified into a few types. To begin with we have plays that are myths of armed resistance on a nationalist basis, with an underpinning of nationalism overriding the theme of class. These are accompanied by the mythification of communist revolution, on revolution, Vietnam, China, Cuba, etc., together with revolutionary insurrections in India where the Communist Party had a central role.

Let us briefly discuss a few of these plays to get a sense of the myths he tries to create. *Titumir*, based on the Farazi uprisings of the 1830s, is one example. This uprising was ruthlessly suppressed by the British administration with the collaboration of their client landlords of the Permanent Settlement in Bengal. Due to their vested interest in the countryside they resented the uprising from among the peasantry, and theur Muslim religious discourse. The Bengali middle class reporting on this struggle in the Calcutta media was extremely negative. Utpal Dutt sought to retrieve this rebellion and its hero Titumir in terms of an anticolonial, antifeudal struggle, expressing the revolutionary aspirations of the people of India. Titumir, the martyred peasant leader, became a prefiguration of a future hero of communist revolution.

In *Tota* (The Bullet), or its other version *Mahabidroh* (The Great Rebellion), we have the defeat of India through the suppression of the Great Rebellion of 1857. In this play also class is less central since the aristocrats and the military leaders join hands with the common people - "sepoys" (soldiers), landless/poor peasants and dispossessed craftsmen - to rid India of the British through an armed struggle. Both the struggle and the defeat are portrayed as heroically tragic. This history of armed struggle is an implicit comment on the actual independence achieved by India, which was not genuinely popular or anti-imperialist. This anger at the nature of Indian independence and regret about the communist party's inability to hegemonize nationalist movement are a constant presence in Utpal Dutt's work - both critical and dramatic.

The other notable play in the context of a historical evocation of national politics is *Kallol* (The Sound of Waves), based on the mutiny in the Royal Indian Navy (1946). This play is also anticolonial and depicts the heroism of the Indian people, particularly through two figures of both sexes, who assume a mythic or a more-than-life-size proportion. Shardul Singh, a gunner of the rebel ship Khyber, and his mother Krishna Bai, go beyond their gendered selves to embody the reason and the spirit of the struggle. Indeed, the ship Khyber in its intransigence is something like the battleship Potemkin in its refusal to surrender.

Among the international historical plays the two plays on the Russian revolution and Vietnam are the most well known. The two former ones on Lenin and Stalin are quite popular in Bengal. This popularity is based mainly on India's long familiarity with both figures and the symbolic status the Russian revolution already holds in India from the time of its occurrence. In these complex plays Utpal simultaneously shows a past victory of socialism in the Soviet Union as a mirror for the present times of bourgeois hegemonic crisis in India. In *Lenin Kothai?* (Where Is Lenin?) the period depicted is between July and October 1917. It marks the underground phase of Lenin during the Kerensky-Menshevik government. The main theme of this play is the betrayal of Lenin by the Mensheviks, raising questions regarding communist alliances with bourgeois reformist or communist revisionist parties. In Stalin 1934 he also takes a short period leading up to the turning point when Stalin emerges as the figure that we later hear of, countering "white terror" with "red terror." In these two plays historicization and political generalizations take place simultaneously. Whereas each period is presented in great detail - lifting for the viewer a few pages out of the history of the Soviet Union, creating dialogue from speeches, congress reports, or texts such as Lenin's State and Revolution - the plays also signal far beyond themselves to the different stages and processes of a revolutionary movement of the working classes everywhere. Lenin and Stalin are Utpal's mythic but personable heroes, particularly Stalin, who is an embodiment of endurance, reason and superhuman sacrifice, driven to a necessary "red terror" through a particular historical conjuncture.

During the Emergency, when direct political criticism became impossible, these historical-political events from abroad offered an Aesopian device for depicting national problems. *Lenin Kothai?* for example is full of contemporary Indian references. An Indian audience immediately recognizes in it the government of Indira Gandhi, and the alliance between Congress (I) and other political parties. The menshevik collusion with Kerensky has a direct parallel with the support offered to Congress (I) by the pro-Soviet, pro-national bourgeoisic CPI, while the Kerensky cabinet echoes with the proceedings in the Indian cabinet. The play was written and performed in this contemporary spirit and understood as such by the audience. *Barricade,* another play written and produced during the Emergency, was based on an incident during the Reichstag fire in Berlin 1933 - as noted in a journal of the time called Unserestrasse. This play again was not only a record of the rise of Nazism in Germany, but on the rise of a type of fascism (according to Utpal Dutt) in India itself. Its plot is similar to a detective story in which the antihero type of character, a naive and honest journalist - a firm believer in the promises of liberal democracy - tries to unravel the mystery of the murder of a major German humanist and philanthropist. This murder has been attributed by the German state to the communists and consequently arrests, detentions and a general smashing of all communist organizations are in full swing. This reporter, of a once-renowned liberal newspaper, finally manages to piece together the puzzle and discloses the nazis as the murderers.

But this is only the surface of the play. For a Bengali audience of the mid-70s, or anyone informed about Congress (I) atrocities in West Bengal during the 1960s and 1970s, there was a very Bengali story hidden within it. It is about the murder of an old and respected liberal progressive political figure - Hemanta Basu - during the pre-Emergency era. It too was blamed on the CPI(M) by the Congress (I) and other right-wing parties. All bourgeois newspapers of Calcutta, Bombay and Delhi advertised it as one more instance of CPI(M), i.e. communist, violence, and an "end of law and order" in the communist-governed state of West Bengal. This led to a veritable witch hunt, murders, bombings on CPI(M) offices, and so on, by youth Congress cadres and sympathizers. The collaboration of the mainstream media was also proved by the fact that they totally ignored the subsequent verdict of the courts which declared the innocence of the CPI(M) cadres. It was proved to be a frame-up by Congress (I). The Bengali audience saw in this play both an

Indian and a German story. The characterization of the newspaper was unmistakeably that of the largest Bengali daily, *Anandabazar Patrika*. The relationship between the editor of this newspaper and the Congress (I) establishment, and its role in communist-bashing in Bengal was familiar to all.

These plays which seek to create myths of armed struggle which are national in character, and sometimes, as with Ajeya Vietnam (Invincible Vietnam), anti-imperialistic, are complemented by plays which seek to create revolutionary myths based on a national and anticolonial culture for the purpose of constructing revolutionary art. We will examine two of these plays in some detail. They are in no way directly political but rather explore the formation of cultural ideological structures in the context of the nineteenth-century colonial Bengal. In particular Utpal Dutt concentrates on the weakening and the obscuring of the Bengali cultural identity vis-a-vis the colonial impact. This necessity of developing an authentic (not original) national cultural identity is posed in terms of the existence of a politics and intellectual life which is the result of the overall hegemonizing effects of colonialism. Acts of cultural reconstruction seen from this perspective become political acts of resistance, and they imply the necessity of the retrieval of the past.

The mythic figure and the revolutionary aesthetic are most developed in *Tiner Talwar* (The Tin Sword) and *Daraon Pathikbar* (Stay Passerby). Utpal Dutt's mythic attempts are concentrated primarily on the nineteenth-century polymathic figure of the poet-dramatist Michael Madhushudan Dutta, who embodied a liberal romantic sociocultural development among the new intelligentsia of Bengal. The biographical trajectory of the hero, not unlike Utpal's or that of other middle-class intellectuals, is constructed in terms of his initial loss of identity in the face of the new colonial bourgeois culture and a subsequent resistance to it through a critical revaluation process and a new aesthetic project. Utpal Dutt recognized the possible revolutionary implication of such a trajectory and synthesized from it the figure of an artist who he saw as rebelling against cultural imperialism. Since imperialismn, cultural and otherwise, is by no means over, this play *Daraon Pathikbar* is meant to give the self-estranged, dehistoricized intelligentsia of Bengal a chance to rethink its own role in developing a national consciousness and a class politics.

The historical accuracy of this play has been questioned. But the issue of historical accuracy is pointless here, because the cultural hero Madhushudan is really less a person than an essential "political truth" that Utpal Dutt constructed. This is the mythical use of history, with a view to capturing the cultural and political developments of Madhushudan's time and of ours. For this purpose, Madhushudan's own life is subordinated to a political representational necessity. Madhushudan, and to a smaller degree, the great educationalist and agitator for women's rights. Ishwar Chandra Vidyasagar, are mirrors in which the Bengali intelligentsia is invited to see its own face. Utpal Dutt gives them to us as our culture heroes and their achievements become the "true myth" of nationalist culture.

The two plays also contain a struggle between a bourgeois colonialist and a revolutionary aesthetic. They promote a spirit of political resistance which is meant to transform bourgeois theatre into a political weapon or tool. The question regarding the relationship between politics and theatre that haunts Utpal from the beginning of his career gropes towards a concrete answer in such plays as *Daraon Pathikbar, Tiner Talwar* or *Ajker Shajahan.* It is implied that political revolutions necessarily entail cultural revolution. This theme is best brought out in Utpal's most well-known play *Tiner Talwar.*

Tiner Talwar was produced for the first time on 12 August 1971 at the Academy of Fine Arts to commemorate one hundred years of Bengali public theatre. It was Utpal Dutt's homage to his theatre ancestors, as well as an attempt to locate the present-day political theatre into a national history, within an older tradition of Bengali theatre. He intended this play to be particularly a tribute to the extraordinary talent, resourcefulness and determination of the nineteenth century playwright-director and actor Girish Chandra Ghosh. Utpal depicted the marginalized middle-class theatre producers of Girish's era as "revolutionaries" who tried to put theatre at the service of the common people and the politics of Bengal, in spite of the constraints placed on them by the owners of the companies and the repression of the colonial state. In Utpal Dutt's own words,

> On the 100th anniversary of Bengali public theatre I bow down to those wonderful people [of theatre] who did not obey the norms of a leprous society and received from it only insult and humiliation - I bow down to those who tore off the masks from the faces of the wealthy even when they existed under the patronage of those collaborators and pimps - I bow down to those who rattled their tin swords in front of the yawning jaws of British brute force and fashioned an image of revolution from the heartache of a conquered people. (Dutt, 1973)

The necessity of creating a politically and socially engaged theatre is introduced in the very first scene of the first act:

Beni: . . . so you don't go to plays?

> Sweeper: Why should I? What's in it for the likes of us any way: The babus (gentlemen) will live it up at the theatres, screw around with women from the market, use language that we can't understand. (*Pours out some dirt.*) Better to watch the dancing girls or Ramlila in our own slum. This peacock Mayur play or whatever that you mentioned - what's it about?
> Beni: Mayurbahan, you see, is the prince of Kashmir. The story -
> Sweeper: Damn the prince! Why do you have to do this? Get all dressed up in your red and blue clothes and tinsels, paint your faces and play at kings and princes? After all this education why must you tie a tin sword around your waist and act childish?
> Beni: Tin sword? Childish?
> Sweeper: Why can't you dress as you are? Can't you see that there is a lot of dirt on you? (Dutt, 1973, p. 2)

Acknowledging that there is a lot of dirt of colonial collaboration on the middle class and a gap between their art and the people, Utpal Dutt tried to dramatize this very problem itself in the play. This crucial question is continued in *Daraon Pathikbar* in asking how to create a people's theatre without entirely discarding what the middle class has created and trained to think of as theatre. In both we find an attempt to solve the problem by producing an example of such a theatre. In *Daraon Pathikbar* the problem is not posed in terms of a contrast between bourgeois and nonbourgeois theatre, but rather of coexistence, where we find that the class lines again merge and there is a mutual appreciation between the producers of people's and bourgeois theatre. The progressive intelligentsia, such as Madhushudan, extend a patronage towards popular entertainment, and a street-theatre group, composed of poor and socially outcast actresses and singers, becomes deeply devoted to the theatre of the progressive bourgeoisie. The private living-room theatres of the landed gentry are shown as being dismantled by playwrights such as Madhushudan and Dinabandhu Mitra and brought out into the streets, among the poor. But it is in *Tiner Talwar* where the issues of revolutionary theatre and theatre aesthetics are explored more deeply. It is here that theatre is situated among the marginal/lumpenized middle classes, and becomes commoditized - a creature of financiers. Here the issue is not one of the coexistence of the two modes, the popular and the bourgeois, but the transformation of entertainment of art theatre into a revolutionary people's theatre.

Tiner Talwar is centred on a nineteenth-century theatre company, The Great Bengal Opera. It is a collage of anecdotes about nineteenth-century theatre, including the story of a trade-off made by Girish Ghosh between the lead actress Binodini in return for a permanent stage (The Star Theatre). The play involves a transformation on three levels. At the level of the individual a woman picked up from the street becomes an artist in her own right. This is similar to Bernard Shaw's *Pygmalion* - in that it is the training of the director-actor Benimadhab (a proxy for Girish Ghosh) which brings about this transformation, which she then claims as her own doing and being. The other is the change of the bourgeois and individualist artist into a politically engaged one. This is achieved when Benimadhab the artist of "pure" theatre and entertainment becomes a political theatre activist in the cause of Swadeshi struggles. Lastly a transformation at the level of art itself, namely that theatre or art changes its reason of existence is used as a tool or weapon for social intervention. The whole theatre group, including the newly created actress herself, changes its view of what theatre is about and for whom.

At the beginning of the play the company is the property of one Birkrishna Daw, who is a broker for an English merchant house and retail trader in scrap iron. Theatre, for him as much a commodity, holds the same value as coal or scrap iron. Theatre's servitude to him or to commerce not only prevents any politicization of theatre itself, but also any attempt at producing intelligent and socially relevant plays. This commercialization ties up theatre both politically and socially because Birkrishna is unwilling to face the anger of the British Raj, by allowing political performances, and to lose the market among hypocritical, canting, puritanical, local high-caste Hindu ruling classes, by allowing the performance of social satires. Faced with this opposition of financiers and "spectator-buyers" Benimadhab transcends into "high" art. But he can never protect himself or his group from constant poverty, humiliation and social rejection. The "purity" of art becomes a puerile dream in the face of capital. But Benimadhab's final inspiration to do political theatre comes from a radical young member of the intelligentsia, a character modeled on Madhushudan. This character actually projects a conflict and a desire within Benimadhab himself.

This dialogue attributed to Priyanath is actually Benimadhab's own and a declaration of war through the medium of theatre:

> As long as our country is under the feet of foreigners, no one can have a moment of relief or rest. When blood of peasants is shed in the great streets of Calcutta - it is my own blood that is drained. A revolutionary soldier murdered in the outskirts of the distant city of Delhi is actually one of my own ribs crushed in my chest. (Dutt, 1973, p. 31)

Fighting against the continuance of disengaged "pure" and "mere" theatre - Benimadhab finally takes the leap in the last act. Throwing away old compromises and fears of loss of patronage and state repression, Benimadhab, in Utpal's words, "jumps into battle with his tin sword - deep into the struggle of the nationalist movement." It is

> a struggle which grows at the end of the battle of Palashi, and which grown through countless armed uprisings of the Indian peasantry whose history is the only real history of India's independence movement. (Dutt, 1977, p. 119)

At the final instance Benimadhab's oppressed theatre challenges colonial brute force to a duel, because

> all the peasants you murdered, all the honour which you robbed from peasant women, the revenge for all of that has gathered here - in my arm. (Dutt, 1973, p. 129)

The tin sword of theatre becomes effective only when empowered by its relationship with popular movement and feeling. It is not difficult to realize that for Utpal this choice that Benimadhab makes should also be that of the present-day Bengali intelligentsia. The reviews of the play show that at least a section of his audience understood that.

So much of the history plays at the level of their story-plots or content. But the task now is to assess their politics or class character. But it is precisely this political character which can not be understood unless we examine the kind of ideological position that informs Utpal's politics in general. The narrative content and formal meditations through which this politics is actualized as theatre must then be examined in relation to the general political reference points. In order to get to this overall political position of Utpal Dutt's Marxism and communism, and relatedly, his aesthetics, politics of representation - both at an aesthetic/dramatic level and that at the level of class - must be treated as two sides of the same project.

A discussion of Utpal Dutt's communism can not happen outside of the context of India's communist movement. He himself says so and emphasizes his direct commitment: "I am partisan, not neutral, and I believe in political struggle. The day I cease to participate in political struggle I shall be dead as an artist too" (Dutt, 1982, p. 34), and proclaims his partisan relationship to the CPI(M). The sole purpose of his theatre, as he sees it, is to move the

Indian communist movement forward.

But this could only be done by initially identifying the needs and weaknesses of the communist movement. This is a difficult task, given the complex determinations of the communist movement in India. The communist movement having originated in a colonial context, with a nationalist movement already in place, its weaknesses and needs were/are in the area of its relationship between nationalism and class politics. The CPI before the split in 1964, and since then both CPI and CPI(M), have sought to introject a class perspective into a bourgeois democratic politics. They have structured themselves between the two strands of parliamentary democracy and the hope of an eventual communist revolution in the future, with the first seen as a stepping stone for the latter. This mixture of liberal tenets and parliamentary democracy and communist revolution is to be found in the Indian left or Marxist movement in general. Like them and his forerunners, the theorists and practitioners of IPTA, Utpal Dutt also tries to negotiate between these two political positions. He also veers between a culturalist, homogeneous, and nationalist reading of the concept of "the people" and that of class. His politics simultaneously works on the possibilities of a broad front of alliance, and an antagonistic class perspective. The concept "the people" and "class" change their content and weight depending on whether they are articulated to a parliamentary united front or a revolutionary politics.

On close scrutiny it becomes apparent that Utpal Dutt's ambition is to create an effective cultural politics by combining nationalism with communism while trying to incorporate within the mixture some features of liberal democracy. Utpal Dutt, is in this a true heir of IPTA. There also we saw the same ambiguous, continuously readjusting relationship between the communist and the nationalist movement and its politically ambivalent use of the concept of "the people" and the frequent supression or subsumption of class in that concept. Utpal Dutt's political theatre finds most ambitious expression in his historic mythic theatre. This national communist theatre is to provide a corrective to Indian independence, to complete an incomplete revolution. This is similar to the attempts of the communist parties to create a hegemony and to complete, as well as recreate, an Indian national revolution on a socialist model.

Many members and associates of IPTA, such as Utpal Dutt, who left IPTA and went on to do their own political work in the areas of theatre and film, are haunted by this thought of an unfinished revolution in India. Utpal Dutt, Bijan Bhattacharya, Ritwik Ghatak, and others continue to ask how it is that the possibilities of a national liberation movement gave away before a liberal nationalist movement, and delivered a government of the bourgeoisie and the landlord? Their plays, films and critical writings address this question and rehearse the era before independence. They particularly question the CPI's relation to the Indian National Congress, and though criticisms which point to the consequences of the Communist Party's surrender to bouregois hegemony, try to close the gap and further the revolutionary process. The bitter criticism against the revisionism of the CPI that fills the pages of Towards a Revolutionary Theatre are more than sectarian vituperations. What, he asks, is the reason for this failure?

According to Utpal Dutt, this failure/collaborationist attitude of the CPI resulted from its inability to sympathize with and organize the overall anticolonial and nationalist sentiments of the Indian "people" and its rejection of armed struggle and fetishization of parliamentary democracy. To this Utpal Dutt adds the so-called ultra-left sectarian line which came down from the CPSU after the 5th Congress and prevented the creation of a national unity. The CPI, having caught up with either trade unionism or parliamentarism, had no project of armed struggle: "Thus grew a gulf between the party of the proletariat and the mainstream of armed struggle in the country" (Dutt, 1982, p. 61). According to Utpal, "The people, everywhere, always, worship armed rebels. They do not sing about Gandhi" (Dutt, 1982, p. 59).

Nation and Class in Communist Aesthetic and the Theatre of Utpal Dutt

In *Towards a Revolutionary Theatre,* Utpal Dutt tries to develop a theory of revolutionary politics and theatre along the line of a specifically Indian and armed revolution. This line is one of balancing the relationship between communism and nationalism and the accomodation within a narrative and theatre form. To create a theatre based on that is the hallmark of political and theatrical realism for Utpal Dutt.

He feels that the specificity and complexity of the state of class struggle in India is such that a political project in general and a political theatre project for India lie in conceiving the agent "the people" as both a class entity and a nonclass national cultural entity. A correct national liberation movement, according to Utpal Dutt, would also have to combine both - simulating a general national cultural movement as well as a class movement. For him a correct party politics and political theatre could only be fashioned along Stalin's prescription for nationalist politics and a revolutionary national culture - that it should be national in form and socialist in content. This sentence in fact functions as a motto for his theatre, and it is Stalin's essay "Marxism and the National Question" that we find the conceptual basis for his epic historical theatre and his guiding principle for constructing a communist movement in India.

More directly influential than Lenin's writings and debates in the Comintern on the same issue, Stalin's position in this document allows us an insight into the formative moment of the communist cultural as well as organizational stance. We can see how from IPTA to now political theatre of Bengal contends with the same issues in almost the same way. We can also see how the aesthetics and politics of representation of communism, from the CPSU (including Lukacs's theories) to Utpal Dutt's theatre, are deeply rooted in the definition of a nation and the political strategies and goals outlined in this text.

We should begin with Stalin's definition of a nation:

A nation is a historically constituted, stable community of people,

> formed on the basis of a common language, territory, economic life and psychological makeup manifested in a common culture. (Franklin, 1972, p. 60)

We can see that while conceptualizing a nation, Stalin's stress is on the elements of commonality, rather than that of division. A nation is seen to be homogeneous, built on the ground of "common culture." It is not seen as a conflicted political entity - riven with class struggle for example - but rather as a "stable community" which has been "historically constituted" through a shared "culture." So while history and culture are important aspects of a nationalist politics, class is not even mentioned. The bases of nationalist politics are cultural rather than economic, and not connected to class exploitation, repression and discontentment. Nationalities or nations as such are discontented when cultural self-determination becomes impossible, "because it [the nation] does not enjoy liberty of conscience (religious liberty)," for instance (Franklin, 1972, p. 80). Politics of nationalism is then a politics that strictly busies itself with rights to self-determination on these "superstructural" grounds.

But in a nondemocratic and colonial/imperialist context such "regional autonomy," or "equal rights of nations" is impossible. In this situation the structural question of class - of politics based on local and foreign capital - becomes paramount and has to be waged before this historical cultural community of a nation can find its own free and equal expression. So what is possible for the minorities or nationalities in the context of a socialist republic such as the USSR is not possible in a colonized India. In such a situation the cultural, historical commonality of a nation, which exists independently from class politics, becomes the agenda for the local aspiring classes which fight foreign occupation and capital. If the bourgeois/landlord classes - the ruling classes - are in ascendancy in national politics, they articulate the nationalist (cultural) issues to their cause. Demands for a political and cultural autonomy become a way to strengthen a bourgeois-landlord hegemony. Class struggle of the proletariat and the peasantry are subsumed within bourgeois nationalism. As Stalin puts it:

> The bourgeoisie of the oppressed nation, repressed on every hand, is naturally stirred into movement. It appeals to its "native folk" and begins to shout about the "fatherland," claiming that its own cause is the cause of the nation as a whole. It recruits itself an army from among its "countrymen" in the interest of . . . the "fatherland." Nor do the

> "folk"always remain unresponsive to its appeals; they rally around its banner; the repression from above affects them to and provokes their discontent. (Franklin, 1972, pp. 67-68)

And also:

> The strength of the national movement is determined by the degree to which the larger strata of the nation, the proletariat and the peasantry, participate in it. (Franklin, 1972, p. 68)

Stalin also outlines the conditions under which bourgeois hegemony develops:

> . . . under the conditions of rising capitalism there is a struggle of the bourgeois classes among themselves. Sometimes the bourgeoisie succeeded in drawing the proletariat into the national movement, and then the national struggle externally assumes a "nationwide" character. But this is so externally. In its essence it is always a bourgeois struggle, one that is to the advantage and profit mainly of the bourgeoisie. (Franklin, 1972, p. 68)

Stalin's statements regarding the situation when other class struggles are hijacked by the bourgeoisie for their own class power actually speaks to the state of affairs in India. In fact Utpal Dutt, and other PWAA and IPTA activists during and after the Indian independence, saw a similar process in action as the Indian National Congress rose to power. They also saw the communist movement failing itself and the people of India. They could agree with Stalin's view that depending on "the degree of development of class-antagonism, on the class consciousness and degree of organization of the proletariat [their Party]," it "rallies to the banner of bourgeois nationalism" or does not (Franklin, 1972, p. 68). They saw the bourgeois takeover being facilitated by "diversions" created by the political presecutions carried on by the English rulers, because the attention "of a large strata" was drawn away from "social questions," to the ones "common" to the proletariat and the bourgeoisie. Then arose notions such as "harmony of interests" across classes, "glossing over the class interest of the proletariat," resulting into "intellectual enslavement of workers" (Franklin, 1972, p. 63).

But whereas Stalin's essay gave an idea as to how nationalist movements should have a clsss thrust in colonial situations, it kept national/cultural issues intrinsically and theoretically separated from, though added to, class issues. Nor did it spell out the particulars of creating a movement in colonized countries which would have a mass and a class character simultaneously. In fact the detailed analysis that he does offer is in the context of the USSR, where the socially and the economically contradictory character of nationalism is actually sought to be diffused by separating out class questions from what he calls "national"/cultural ones. Commonality is the element that is stressed as a feature of national groups, and the analysis always veers towards a cultural rather than a structural question, thereby creating two related but separate spheres. Nor does Stalin offer an insight into the question of how to create a "proletarian" struggle when the industrial working class is very small and the peasantry predominates. In this use too, the category "the people" (a key word in nationalist movements), continuously slips from a class connotation, which divides the national terrain, into one of cultural, linguistic, religious, creative-cultural commonness and unites by over-riding or subsuming many of the class elements.

A communist programme that unites these two aspects of national and class politics is to be found in the CPI(M)'s programme of People's Democratic Revolution (PDR), which finally rests upon the proletariat (in the shape of the Party) the task of completing the project of the bourgeois revolution and enlightenment, and sees the projects of class and nation as compatible. Utpal Dutt fully subscribes to the PDR. It is the key to his epic aesthetics. For this reason he has been accused of political opportunism. But if we look at the thrust of Utpal's work from its very first stage, we can see the coincidence of liberal democracy with class struggle, which is the CPI(M) project. The Peoples Democratic Revolution, as he understands it, clarifies for him as a cultural producer the task of a theatre activist in the present political situation. We should attend to two statements in which he accurately presents the basic politico-cultural projects of the PDR:

> . . . but I doubt if revolutionary practices of the theatre have worked out what this [Peoples Democratic Revolution] implies in terms of battle for people's minds. I doubt if many of us have realized that this means that many of the slogans in such a revolution will be inherited from the great bourgeois-democratic revolutions of Europe, but since the semi-colonial bourgeoisie is incapable of raising them, the proletariat must take up the task and with the help of other revolutionary class, fulfill the democratization of the country. And since the proletariat must exercise hegemony in this revolution, it is no longer a bourgeois democratic revolution, which is part of the world-socialist revolution. But its content will be democratic and therefore related to, for example, the

thoughts of the Great French Revolution of 1789. (Dutt, 1982, p. 64)

Where a people's democratic revolution will differ from the revolutionary ideas of Diderot and Rousseau will precisely be where the revolutionary bourgeois thinkers halted in confusion, where they became scared by their own honest findings, and instead of pursuing their own logic, sought to find compromise, within the framework of bourgeois society. The proletarian democratic revolution is aimed at finally smashing that framework, and therefore will not halt, but pass onto the next stage, a socialist revolution. (Dutt, 1982, p. 64)

We should carefully attend to the statement that the content of Indian communist revolution "will be inherited from the great bourgeois revolution," realize the "ideas of Diderot and Rousseau" and be "related to the Great French Revolution of 1789." However, it will be the task of "the proletariat" to "fulfil the democratization of the country," though of course "with the help of other revolutionary classes." And in the next stage - after ushering in an era of enlightenment and establishing a parliamentarian democratic framework - the proletariat "will not halt, but pass onto the next stage, a socialist revolution." PDR is meant as the culmination of the incomplete revolution - the genuine independence that bypassed India. This position can be directly related to a sentence from Stalin, which featured on the walls of Calcutta during the Stalin centenary year: "The banner of bourgeois democracy lies in the dust today, the proletariat must pick it up and carry it forward." Under this banner proletarian and bourgeois theatre can surely coexist side by side, as can socialism and class harmony.

We should note how the PDR and a Stalinist or Second Internationalist politics allows for the possibility of retainment of bourgeois culture. This is the result of both considering the bourgeoisie, and in particular European boureoisie, as a revolutionary class, and culture in a nonmediatory relationship with class. These views allow Utpal Dutt to hold an admiration for two strident extremes of theatre/literature and even find a reconciling principle among them. He can admire and emulate high bourgeois culture and speak of class struggle, or use agit-prop forms, all at once. He assumes that the bourgeois literature of one era can be the legacy of, serviceable to, the proletariat of the next. These positions are overtly demonstrated, in plays such as *Daraon Pathikbar,* where these antagonistic classes can come to an easy, spontaneous collaboration with each other, in which "the people" find a natural leader (not just an ally), for instance in Madhushudan or Vidyasagar, in the bourgeoisie, who leads them on to a national struggle - in this instance a cultural struggle against colonialism. The use of the two categories, "the people" and class, in this play shows clearly the problems involved in synthesizing a dual politics - where relations between class and culture, revolution and bourgeois democracy remain unsettled but constant. Again in *Tiner Talwar* we find a similar reworking of the concepts of the people and revolution. Whereas in most of his other plays the spectrum includes workers and peasants, here with the exception of the first five minutes of the play, where a sweeper is instructed to us, "the people" are the theatre people of the nineteenth-century stage. This redifinition of "the people" and the politics of cultural nationalism speaks more of a cultural revolution under the leadership of the petty bourgeois intelligentsia than an armed class struggle. If it results in an armed struggle at all, it is more likely to be annexed to a bourgeois national venture than one of a class struggle and the victory of the proletariat.

Utpal Dutt: An Assessment

Political subjects in themselves do not make political theatre . . . you can have a play dealing with racism, or sexism, or fascism, and if the subject is dealt with in, let's say, an Ibsen-like way, then the audience is left with nothing to do in working on the problem, you might just as well read about the subject in a newspaper. That is not political theatre.

EDWARD BOND, interview in Plays and Players

A bourgeois theatre and a revolutionary project can well go together, if culture can be abstracted from class. The coherence between a Stalinist political project which separates class from culture and a bourgeois nationalist theatre aesthetic will become evident as we discuss the epic historic theatre of Utpal Dutt, with its core of mythic realism. This aesthetic project can be directly traced to the socialist epic-myth project developed by Maxim Gorky in the Stalinist era. We should take note of Gorky's statement at the very beginning of our discussion:

> Any myth is a piece of imagining. Imagining means abstracting the fundamental idea underlying the sum of a given reality, and embodying it in an image; that gives us realism. But if the meaning of what has been abstracted from reality is amplified through the addition of the desired and the possible - if we supplement it through the logic of hypothesis - all this rounding off the image - then we have the kind of romanticism which underlies the myth, and is most beneficial in its prompting a revolutionary attitude toward reality, an attitude that in practice refashions the world. (Gorky, p. 323)

The inspiration for Utpal Dutt's serious political theatre lies in the Stalinist politics discussed in the previous part and statements such as these. In fact he is a self-confessed Stalinist. He wrote two plays in homage to Stalin, *Louha Manab* (The Man of Iron) and *Stalin 1934*. And also in Stanislavsky Theke Brecht, for example, he discusses the Stalinist base of his own epic philosophy:

> In the question of form there is nothing that is the greatest or the ultimate. Formula is the death of drama. Moreover according to Stalin the form always has to be national, the content socialist. Every nation [jati] has created its favourite forms for many centuries. It will want to see its revolutionary theatre in those very forms. Perhaps the revolutionary message will reach the Japanese quickest if put through kabuki, to the people of Bengal in jatra, and in South India through dance, in Maharashtra in tamasha, in Uttar Predesh in nautanki, in Gujarat through bhawai. The main issue is thr revolutionary content. The form is dependent on a country and time, content is eternal. (Dutt, 1982a, p. 82)

We can see from the quotation how Utpal assumes, as did Stalin and others, a commonality of culture at the level of the nation (jati) - both in ideas and forms of art, as well as in the separation between form and content. In their view national culture is assumed to be homogeneous and can over-ride divisions such as that of class and manifest in a body of unified, shared images, forms and ideas. To create a theatre that can thus capture the so-called spirit of a nation and an age through its form, and direct it towards the content of a communist revolution, is the historical mission of Utpal Dutt's political theatre.

In order to create a theatre which projects a commonality and builds a national theatre, and fuses or overrides the divisions of a class society and yet accomodate class struggle, Utpal Dutt resorts to the notion of epic. Its end is to produce both national and proletarian myths to further a communist revolution. As we have seen in the previous section, it consists of mythicization and apotheosis, i.e., the fixation and enlargement of particular historical individuals and events in history. In order to put together such a governing aesthetic and a representational apparatus Utpal Dutt draws upon various and disparate indigeneous and foreign sources. His sources range from Indian epics to bourgeois Bengali and European literature and mythopoeic attempts by nationalist and revolutionary writers, especially from Germany and the

USSR. Though following Brecht and Piscator, and probably in order to give it a socialist context and legitimacy, he also called it "epic theatre," but Utpal's epic theatre is not the epic theatre of either of these dramatists. His epic theatre typically suits his own, a combination of an Indian and a Soviet style, politics.

In order to get to the heart of Utpal Dutt's politics, and since the concept of epic theatre has become identified with the theatre of Brecht, it is important to differentiate his theatre project from Brecht's epic theatre. It is far more revealing of his own epic aesthetic and practice than that of Brecht. Here is his version of Brecht's intentions for constructing the epic form.

> After much thinking Brecht came to this conclusion, that showing too many emotions all together creates too much complication in the play. It creates confusion in an ordinary audience in understanding the theory of revolution. On the other hand as a Marxist, as a dialectician, it was impossible for him to think of man as purely white or black. His epic convention was a discovery to create a solution to this problem or we might say that it was a rediscovery. As he took from the ancient epics an analytical and distancing perspective, he also supplied the answer to the question of "how shall I show man?" from that very ancient epic. Shakespeare's characters become increasingly more complex from scene to scene, but that never happens in the ancient epics. Arjun or Karna are never mentally agitated, they are great and tranquil as stone sculptures. In each canto they show different emotions. Arjun is sometimes a lover, sometimes a great warrior, and sometimes averse to war . . . This does not wait for so-called logic. An epic, because it distances itself, is not locked within an everyday life. As we don't need a worldly logic for legends, so for epics. Brecht has reestablished this form in the light of modern science, and conferred on to theatre the greatness of legends and the nobility of the epic. Courage is sometimes a mother, sometimes a cunning trader, sometimes a satirist of the feudal warmonger, sometimes bewildered and stupid . . . All these, all together, slowly create the whole human being. Courage in the audience's imagination. (Dutt, 1982a, pp. 80-81)

Dutt's version of Brecht is actually a mirror of his own work. Brecht himself was not interested in a display of emotions - neither in "too many all at once" nor sequentially - nor in creating characters with depth - "the whole human being"and certainly not in "greatness" and "nobility." In fact if we return to the chapter on realism we will immediately see that Brecht's interest in the epic form had nothing to do with its content of stories of heroic deeds of heroic men and their battles or historic, imperial missions. Unlike Utpal, he did not believe that they form the content of the cultural unconscious of Europe or that there was such a homogeneous cultural unconscious. Brecht used the epic form for the exact opposite reason of Dutt, namely, to create distance and alienation - as a narrative form with which the European audiences of his time had very little connection. It was a major device for the "alienation effect." This alienation effect gave the distance required by the audience and author alike for a critical and a "logical" representation of contemporary reality. So it was the form - the nonlinear, but not illogical, narrative structure - and not the content that interested Brecht in epics. He saw the epic structure as choppy, with self-contained episodes, each with its own life and logic. Through the use of this device he sought to destroy what might be called a singular focus or a perspective view on reality on theatre. Decentred in this way, the pieces of episodes, possible actions and options, could only form a whole dramatic structure as a set of social and critical relations with each other. The text was held together by these relations, and not through an internal, cause-and-effect sequence of events or emotional connections, or through any primary episode governing the others. His interest was in actively critical and mediatory relations between the parts, as well as between the play and the audience. Meaning was gained from referring the episodes and their relations within the play to a social reality and a social analysis that lie outside the text. The socialist/communist politics of a play such as *Mother Courage and her Children* or *Galileo* for example cannot be found in its story or dialogue - in any of the characters, events, or decisions - but rather in a series of provocative textual disjunctures and in the audience-text conjunction, which prompts one to think exactly the very opposite of what is going on on the stage. The need for breaking the old Aristotelian unities of time, space and action, in short a political and formal opposition to hundreds of years of theatre of property and the bourgeoisie made Brecht gravitate towards the epic form.

Utpal Dutt on the other hand does not want to operate within the Brechtian tradition of alienation and criticality. He has only a limited formal interest in epics, and makes no use of their discursive episodic structure, which Brecht used in order to insert political comments and social analysis. Utpal's comments on Brecht's particular use of epics offer us a point of entry for discussing his own:

The amazing thing is that Brecht held up to us arrogantly the reverse of

> what people always understood the epic-hero to be. Brecht is suspicious of an earth shaking under heroic trade. Only unfortunate countries need heroes. *Courage* and *Galileo* both say this. Brecht's heroes are dwarfs in social life. Brecht has created the fantasy world of epic and unleashed in it a bunch of kicked aroundm selfish little creatures, who think it's heroic to cheat others and survive. Brecht's epic is also a cruel satire of the ancient epics. His plays are not epics - but at once the re-establishment of it. (Dutt, 1982a, p. 136)

Utpal's interest in epics is in their content, in the masculine and the heroic, and in terms of exaggerated emotions, large-scale characterization and scope of action. Unlike Brecht, with his interest in distancing and alienation, Utpal's intention is to create a theatre of absorption through what he considers to be a common national heritage. According to Dutt the ancient epics - the *Mahabharata* and the *Ramayana* - are a part of "our national psyche." Trapped in this notion of a common heritage, he sees no distinction between how they are understood or used by the different classes, or in the cities and the countryside of Bengal and India. In fact, it is the perception and use of the Indian epics by his nineteenth-century middle-class ancestors that provides him with the basis and the perspective for the project of a national, cultural united front for politics. Heroism of both action and character, multiple incidents, and great battles are what he selects out of the epic's content. This use of epics is a characteristic of nineteenth- and twentieth-century history plays and urbanized commercial jatra. These features are also coherent with Utpal's own interest in Shakespeare and Elizabethan plays. Furthermore, unlike for Brecht, emotional absorption and excitement rather than criticality is the heart of Utpal's epic-mythic project. The epic, for him, is a matter of grand passion.

Utpal Dutt reworks the epic form and scope into a bourgeois play, with plots and subplots, many scenes, heroic characters and incidents. He changes its episodic structure into a linear dramatic pattern by introducing a single overriding action and focus, mounting emotionality and an internal sequence of regulating causality in a manner resembling fate. The Aristotelian unities reappear in either a modified or a direct way and contribute to the tale and the fate of one hero. Unlike Brecht's, Utpal's epic hero is constructed without irony, and the play revolves on his "action" - i.e. on his success or failure as the plot centres on some world-shattering event, rather than on the trivia of capitalism that occupies Brecht. It is in his own theatre that we get an insight into when he discovers a "hero" (or antihero), "characters" in the sense of the word the individual and "a quest for a whole man" in either the epics or

Brecht's plays, and moreover finds them compatible with Shakespearean inner conflicts. This is why he can erroneously deduce that Brecht used the epics in a sequence of actions and emotions to create a "rounded character" as A C Bradley said of Shakespeare or that he sought "to create a whole man" out of fragmentary experiences. (Dutt, 1982a, p. 124) His own plays are created on a totalist view of reality, as for instance prescribed by Lukacs, with an intact and sequentially organized surface, rather than as a set of intersecting social relations.

We must remind ourselves at this point that the politics of Brecht's theatre and Utpal's differ substantially. Utpal Dutt's epic theatre, unlike Brecht's epic theatre for class struggle, is first and foremost a nationalist theatre with an added on rather than an intrinsic socialist agenda. Its purpose, as he himself points out, is not mainly to teach a critical class perspective, but rather to incite the audience to class hatred and armed political action with an assumption that the audience knows all it needs to know about class and the appropirate emotions pertaining to "class characters." Though Bharucha sees box-office as the sole motive behind the emotionalism of his plays, there is actually a political reason which is far more relevant:

> It is a proven fact that if we want to explain the rules of social change Brecht's technique is the best. But for a Marxist, to explain is not the only task, but also to incite, to promote class-hatred, to "instill in the audience's subconscious a lack of faith in the bourgeois social organization. (Lenin, "What is to be Done?" Dutt, 1975, p. 48))

For Utpal Dutt a revolutionary theatre can only be created through introducing great feelings, which inspire the audience to look beyond its petty lives into heroic exploits and sentiments, which in turn move it beyond "the so-called logic of our daily world and "refashion," as Gorky said, "our attitude to reality." The path of this popular revolutionary theatre for Utpal lies through the land of history, legends and the heroic:

> . . . the petty-bourgeois writers and directors will never find content in the cul-de-sac of their own class. If they wish to survive as artists, they must listen to the screams, howls and songs issuing from the new Elsinore, watch new *Hamlets* and *Lohengrins* set out on a mission of setting right a world out of joint, confront new tragedies, taking massive shape just outside the petty bourgeois hovels.
>
> To create new tragedies, new heroes and their violence against new villains, the artist must acquire by choice the standpoint of the class that

> is making new history - namely the proletariat. (Dutt, 1982, pp. 104-5)

It is melodrama with its steep ups and downs of passion rather than epic that serves his theatre in its revelation of what he calls the "mythic" or essential reality. He reads just such a melodrama into Goethe's *Faust* (Part I), and in his reading he finds a suitable form and vision. According to Dutt, while the inside of Faust encases the zeitgeist of a capitalist Germany, its significance becomes universal for all of capitalism by the use of the form of melodrama which surpasses the "realistic" level, with ghosts, witches, and black magic . . . including . . . horror. (Dutt, 1982, p. 131)

The ultimate purpose of Utpal's epic theatre is to create "myths," rather than question or work with the ones which already exist. Myths for him are characterized and fictionalized "essences" or "truths" - they are the product of the highest kind of realism. The literary method of this mythic realism is obviously not naturalism, but even its epistemology is not concerned with the actually existing everyday life. It is through a transcendence of the particular, of daily life, and historical and social time and space that his epic-mythic theatre is sought to be created. His epic-mythic ideals are worth recounting in this context. In his essay on "form of theatre," in TART he makes the following statements:

> A myth is a poetic summary of a people's collective experiences. It is the signature of a whole historical epoch . . .
> A myth transposes time because it has nothing to do with "realism" in the vulgar sense.
> It aims at the super-real and therefore remains true in different contexts, in different versions. (Dutt, 1982, pp. 131-132)

The mythic therefore has to be not only artistic and artificial but also idealist in its conception of a temporality. Neither the "essential" truth about reality nor the creation of true art is possible for him by staying close to what he calls "life." It comes out most clearly in *Stanislavskir Path* when, assessing his favourite actor and director, he states both his and Stanislavsky's theatre ideal:

> Art is not created through an imitation of life. Acting is not a parody of a man seen on the street. Acting is life-transcending, a harmonious expression that rises above life. (Dutt, 1975, p. 23)

In this kind of statement we see the coming together of a purely idealist version of truth and art with a political aim, that purports to be communist/socialist and effect historical social changes within a distinctly temporal dimension.

The mythic-epic attempt is meant to capture a whole people's collective experience (it is the national ideal again) as though such an experience were possible in actuality, rather than those of certain classes, and thus both appeals to and creates a commonality. It is interesting that along with this a temporal, essentialist project Utpal Dutt can talk at once about the importance of history. He speaks of "transcending time," of art being "super-real" and "true in different contexts" as well as socialist/communist revolution in the same breath. In order to establish a baseline that holds for all, Utpal Dutt ends up by eradicating the very contemporaneity and specificity which he holds characteristic of a nonabstract, "non-quixotic" political theatre.

These totalist epic ventures lack as yet, for Utpal, a fully accomplished form or a model. In TARI he tells us that he has to break a new path:

> The proletariat myths have not been created. The proletarian revolution has not produced its Goethe and Schiller yet. There are historical reasons for it . . . the proletariat [however] under the bourgeois, is reduced to the level of a cretin, except for a handful of labour aristocrats, who, being puppets to be used against the proletariat, no longer remains proletarian. (Dutt, 1982, p. 133)

He turns for hints and models to the established European bourgeois of Bengali nationalist (also bourgeois) theatre. He finds in Shakespeare the most relevant structure of characterization for the mythic-epic. In *Shakespeare Samaj Chetana* (Shakespeare's Social Consciousness) he speaks of Shakespeare's dramatic structures and characters - heroes and villains - that can embody "the spirit of the age" in "mythic" figures such as that of Hamlet. In *Hamlet* and *King Lear*, for example, he finds a total embodiment, a complete man, not to be found anywhere else except in the epics.

But Utpal reserves his greatest praise for Richard Wagner for creating "a new myth, a revolutionary Holy Grail, a poetic reinterpretation of the oldest ballads in North European memory." (Dutt, 1982, p. 109) After discussing the operas he says that Wagner's great achievement was "to marshal the knight, armour and all, to the service of revolutionary bourgeois ideology." (Dutt, 1982, p. 106)

Among the Bengali theatre producers and playwrights he credits Girish

Gosh for having tried a mythopoeic theatre. But compared to Shakespeare, Goether, Schiller and Wagner, he feels Girish's work is a failure - "his outlook was probably vitiated by an unwarranted veneration for his heroes." (Dutt, 1982, p. 140) Utpal blames a historical determination for this failure since colonialism prevented India from producing either a bourgeois or a proletarian revolution. "Naturally no myth, proletarian and bourgeois, has been created in India in the field of art and literature." (Dutt, 1982, p. 139) He also relies on the dramatized versions of epical stories in jatra and the historical and mythological plays. These modified examples of early or precapitalist theatre are considered by him as India's only valid and substantive sources of heroism and grand visions necessary for constructing myths. They are the Indian counterparts of the bourgeois heroic myths of Europe, and reconcilable within the same text.

It is interesting that whereas Utpal Dutt spends such time discussing bourgeois playwrights and directors, such as Wagner, who had a mythic project without an interest in socialism and a "folkism" without any class content, he spends less time on a socialist playwright who also wanted to create proletarian myths. Though he alludes to Maxim Gorky periodically, produced The Lower depths and used Gorky's advocacy of imagination as the way to truth to legitimize his own mythic project, he discusses him only cursorily, and finally even negatively. After many pages on the successes of of Richard Wagner as creator of a genuine popular revolutionary myth in the legends of Siegfried, Lohengrin, Parcifal, etc., later providing the mythology of German National Socialist Party, he mentions Gorky only to inform us that he had failed in his mythic project due to his "revolutionary romanticism." Gorky was, in contrast to Wagner, for example, "too involved in his hero's fate, too sympathetic to the hero's goal." (Dutt, 1982, p. 134)

This assessment of Gorky is very intriguing. The fact is that Utpal's own project to create a national and revolutionary theatre, at the service of contemporary communist politics in a classically romantic mode, was most clearly formulated by Maxim Gorky in an effort of socialist construction in the USSR. This becomes evident from the 1934 Writers Congress held in the USSR. And furthermore a similar directive presence of particularly Lenin's, and Stalin's thought also shapes the course of Gorky's literary philosophy and forms of production. Gorky was well known in India and there were many translations of his novels, plays and stories. His literary theories were also well known and much debated.

In TART it is actually in the few allusions to Gorky that we find the parallel of another literature and theatre that is both socialist and romantic. Put in another way, it is in the project of socialist realism, with its core of revolutionary romanticism, that we find a European version of the aesthetic of the mythic-epic theatre of Utpal Dutt. Socialist realism of this type allows a blend of revolutionary nationalist theatre of urban Bengal (from Girish Gosh to Sachin Sengupta), urbanized jatra and the progressive bourgeois literature/theatre of the West. It is in Gorky that Utpal Dutt gets his theory of myth, of a romantic political theatre which captures truth through imagination and exaggeration, rather than in the critical realism of the older socialist project. Feelings and national cultural myth and symbols become the staple of this art. As he calls his theatre "epic" to situate it in a genealogy of political theatre, so too he used Gorky's definition of myth to legitimize hos own practice:

> As Maxim Gorky explained Myth, it is not idle imagination or pure fabrication but a glorified, exagerrated statement of a very real problem of the ancient world. (Dutt, 1982, p. 113)

Gorky's mythic project was simple and grand. He talked of a mythic work as being "a piece of imagining," "abstracting the fundamental idea," and "embodying it in an image." Contrary to what had so far been claimed as realism, this active exercise of the imagination, he claims, "gives us realism." But it is not the realism of daily life that surrounds us, rather "reality is amplified," "supplemented" by "the logic of hypothesis." This excursion into what does not yet exist, hitherto negatively branded as "escapist," fantastic and romantic by both positivist and critical communism, had now become important for the work of revolutionary construction of the USSR. Stalin himself had endorsed romanticism as did cultural theorists such as Zhdanov, Radek and Bukharin as indicated by the 1934 Congress. But, as pointed out by Gorky in his essay "Advice to Young Writers," this romanticism was not considered "bourgeois" - consisting of decadence, despair and degeneracy - but rather "revolutionary." "The kind of romanticism which underlies the myth" is aimed towards "promoting a revolutionary attitude towards reality." "In practice," it "refashions the world." "Romanticism" for Gorky "is an active attitude towards life. (Gorky, p. 41)

We have discussed so far how at the level of content and construction of his plays and theatre philosophy Utpal Dutt tries to create a "popular" and "revolutionary" theatre in accordance with a Stalinist political programme of a People's democratic Revolution. In this section we will examine his use of various theatre styles and forms in order to find a language for the full range of his political theatre. We must remember that he has to produce theatre for an immediate pragmatic and daily business of the Communist

Party, trade unions and provincial politics - as much as for his epic-mythic history project. As the purpose and the content varies, so must the form. Since from our standpoint politics and theatre are irreducible mediating components of each other, we must explore the form-content relationship in his work. Though Utpal himself, in the following quotation for example, separates out "the message" or "the content" from the form, and feels that the content remains uncompromised in its dress of whatever form "pleases" the audience, we ourselves can not adopt this attitude:

> The director belched: "No Sir, why? Why should I put cheap and reactionary material on my stage? Whoever told you that whatever is stateable and popular is cheap and vulgar?
>
> The playwright was pacing in intolerable rage.
>
> Continuing his pacing he asked: "So what does popular or stateable really mean?"
>
> The director picked his teeth with a matchstick and said: "I don't know about other theatres; maybe there they do use the audience as an excuse for showing cheap things, like the Bombay movie directors do. But I have faith in myself. It's impossible to bring any reactionary material in my theatre while trying to make it stateable. And yet, the play must have such tension, such speed, such surprise that the audience must get real pleasure from it, so that they won't boycott my theatre. I don't compromise at all on the count of content. I maintain the playwright's progressive message absolutely intact, because I am also a progressive man. But that message, that content must appear in front of the audience, set up on the stage with such styles and techniques, that the audience can understand, appreciate, be pleased with it. Otherwise what will happen - just this, that even a strong message will appear in a nonunderstandable form, and no one will get it. The message is then completely lost. Formal experiments can never discount the question of the audience. (Dutt, 1979, pp. 25-26)

Whether Utpal Dutt's theatre politics furthers a revolutionary goal or not must therefore be answered in the context of a taken-for-granted set of theatre mediations, which constitute a part of the common sense of the theatre-going and -producing Bengali middle class. This element of class subjectivity, expressed through the form, is a vital one in any study of politics of art.

We already know that an interest in both a national culture and class politics governs Dutt's theatrical choice and experiments. He is simultaneously theatrically pragmatic and ideologically dogmatic. What his audience is familiar with - the national tradition of bourgeois theatre - becomes the vehicle of his politics. After all, as Utpal says, even "a terribly strong message" could also be "lost" if the audience could not read it in the theatre's text nor relate it to any of their previous theatre experiences. It is for this reason, not simply out of a commercial interest, that he says, "Formal experiments can never discount the question of the audience" (Dutt, 1982a, p. 95). As this politics tries to combine divergent ideological strands into one, so it does with divergent theatre traditions. Hence his search through both national and internationsl repertoire. His theatrical eclecticism is a practical dimension of his political necessity. His search for form, and his formal combinations, are devices for presenting his politics effectively. What he sees as the ideal Marxist/communist stand in the matter of formal experimentation, we find in the following remark on Brecht:

> There should be no obligation to obey any convention because it is established, nor should there be a reluctance to use it because it is an old convention. After all Brecht's theatre is political theatre, its politics must reach the people. This is the only intention of his theatre. Those who sit on judgement on Brecht's theatre using the criteria of aesthetics, are as though judging a 25-inch cannon as a thing of beauty. A political theatre can not be encompassed within an aesthetics any more than armaments can be. Political theatre operates with only one condition - whether the politics is accurately reaching the audience. One must do whatever is necessary for that. Brechtian techniques - alienation and surprise - are the creation of a political necessity. (Dutt, 1982a, p. 95).

What we want to do then is not to explain away the seemingly antithetical aspects of Utpal's theatre and politics, but put side by side the form and the politics, and we will see, as we did in the previous section, why it is that these old bourgeois playwrights proved to be of such interest and a source of influence for him or why antithetical forms and contents can cohabit without producing a sense of contradiction. We found that the epic-mythic quest is largely suited to a national and bourgeois cultural quest - and not a part and parcel of a proletarian theatre. Instead of positing an unqualified contradiction between the European bourgeois or older nationalist theatre of Bengal and Utpal's own theatre, it would perhaps be more fruitful to ask what they have in common politically, so that his formal affinity and attitude to those theatres may be better understood. And furthermore we should remember that Utpal considers theatre to be an art and the purpose of art as being to produce pleasure consisting of a small core of instruction and a great deal of passion. Unlike Brecht, who also brought pleasure into the theatre, but insisted that it be of learning, Dutt does not equate the two. For him the message can come dressed in many forms. He is not particularly concerned about the problems that the message can get into, or be transformed into, as a result of the dresses or the forms. We have to question, then, why or how he can afford to overlook theatrical mediation's ability to mediate the politics of theatre.

Utpal Dutt is not only convinced that theatre is an art, but he is also a proponent of an ostentatious, self-conscious theatre art, of what Grotowski calls a "rich theatre," (Dutt, 1979, p. 112) meaning a theatre that uses a proscenium stage and draws upon many other arts, disciplines and technology to enrich itself. Multiple forms and techniques combine to create his language of theatre, the less austere the better. Utpal sees theatre as an art that is synthetic, polymorphic and synaesthetic. Asking the question, "But where are the rules for theatre? Where is its grammar, its lexicon?" (Dutt, 1979, p. 112) he proceeds to list the elements of theatre, namely the actor with his dialogue, gestures and movement, and the stage design, light and music. Theatre is "promiscuous," an attempt to unite what we hear and see. "Isn't there such a ground at all where visuals and music, dance and words, without losing their integrity, sit at the same table?" With the proper daring, daring to be both artificial and artistic, one could create "a theatre which was the combined creation of many arts . . . where sound can become colour, and colour sound" (Dutt, 1979, p. 112). Needless to say, with such an opulent view of theatre as a "total" art, whose "muse" is "proud, queenly and resplendent" Utpal Dutt is an ennthusiast of the proscenium stage. (Dutt, 1979, p. 54)

The theatre taste that derives from the last one hundred years of Bengali urban, professional stage is the staple ot Utpal Dutt's theatre. The world of professional and traditional stage become Utpal's natural habitat and at no point in time could he conceive of politics in any other way except theatrically, but nor did he ever attempt a theatre from which he did not glean a political service of sorts. But Utpal Dutt's standard remained the old proscenium stage, which has become identified with theatre proper. An elevated box stage with curtains, with inner stages, wings, revolving sets, light and amplification, this is the stage of mainstream theatre in front of which generations of audiences have waited for the thrill of the curtain to rise since the beginning of the national theatre era in Bengal. With some variations in its internal organization, Utpal Dutt has mounted all his full-length plays on this stage and written them with this stage in mind. The stage directions in his printed texts point to stage environment, devices of organizing, varying and speeding up the action, all of which clearly show the centrality of the stage as an organizing principle of dramatic representation. Not only are there frequent changes of scene through the use of curtains, but also the role of light (in spotlighting acting zones by using certain colours of light and darkening the other areas) is similar and as well signifies levels of reality within the play.

Utpal Dutt's stage is mainly a direct descendent of nineteenth-century colonial, and by extension, bourgeois commercial European stage. In fact in its fullness of decor, sound and light, and excessiveness of emotions, it has an old-fashioned Victorian touch to it. It lacks the severity of a modernist or postmodernist stage. It is not the sparse stage of Brecht, nor the denuded stage of the theatre of the absurd. Nor is the naturalistic stage of the drawing-room theatre. It is a little too stuffed, too warm, often it conjures up the aura of red velvet stage furniture, gilded mirrors, or epic battle fields - no matter where they are - be they in Vietnam or the plains of Hindustan. It is however productive of illusions which quite openly suggest its own theatricality and separate reality. The use of painted scenes, not just objects and platforms that constitute space-time relations within a play, is still prevalent as are heavy and manifold props, and certainly used consciously by Utpal Dutt when producing plays on nineteenth-century Bengali theatre and life. This stage, in short, is a highly "theatrical" stage - and is modified to suit different types of his theatre.

Utpal Dutt's contribution to this stage has been to raise its theatricality or artificiality even higher than usual within the IPTA left theatre heritage. It is meant to create an environment for his mythic-epic theatre. The stage for epic theatre, with a high quantity of advanced theatre technology and techniques which elevate it to an "epic" or grand scope level, could not have been possible in the days of Girish Gosh. The productive forces of their days were far lower, but now it is entirely possible to create a theatre where one not only hears dialogue but sees spectacles and hears music and other sound effects. With Utpal Dutt the element of the spectacular dominates as a part of the epic-mythic expression - though there are also productions where he uses some features of the epic style to be found in Brecht and Piscator. In those plays the stage-scope is used to supply information and suggest complexity of action - though the attempt remains mainly that of developing a story linearly.

Along with the influence of theatre proper both from Europe and Bengal, Utpal Dutt uses the indigenous urbanized dramatic tradition of jatra, as well as forms such as street theatre and agit-prop. Utpal Dutt's use of jatra however has not moved him away from the use of the proscenium and its general format. After all, it is not the rural version of jatra with its open platform stage that he draws on. In terms of textual construction perhaps Utpal Dutt has been more interested in the traditional mythological jatra with its morality plot, great battles, gods and goddesses, kings and queens, than the austere nonmythological, social jatras of the nationalist Mukunda Das. Utpal Dutt's own jatras are not distinguishable from his historical plays.

Because "epic" theatre has to juggle with such diverse elements, the question of balancing or synthesizing them becomes an important one. The principle of balance or synthesis becomes evident in Utpal's work as a director, even more than as a playwright. The "dramatic action" is not only the story which Utpal retells, but a plot, and its staged form, in which the representation takes its complete shape. The directorial work consists of what is called the "composition" of a show - its technique of "mounting." The particulars of the composition come as much from the types of theatre the director prefers as from his politics. In fact the plays are written by many playwrights with the composition in mind. A model for Utpal's theatre is to be found in his version of Kshirod Prasad Vidyavinod's play *Alamgir.* It is here, in a nationalist, big stage production, that we discover the key to Utpal's technique of dramatizing the epic. In his ideal model of composition of a play the following elements are essential:

> 1) The speed of the action, i.e., the organization of the events should make the audience breathless. There should be parallel actions, which are exciting as well.
> 2) The events should be unusual and surprise the audience continually.
> 3) There should be rapid change of mood as well as events.
> 4) There should be liberal use of humour - to satirize as well as please.
> 5) There should be a "dramatic" development of characters.

Nothing is too dramatic for the purpose of the epic stage:

> The expression "over-dramatized" is meaningless. Dramas are meant to be dramatic - pitched at an octave higher than life. Where massive personalities are clashing with each other, empires are rising or falling, how can any incident seem "over-dramatic"? (Dutt, 1979, p. 30)

How Utpal himself learnt from his predecessors becomes evident from the organization of the play *Tiner Talwar.* Here we see that same perfection in split-second timing, rapid rise and fall in moods, flow of action, surprise and humour which have been the envy of other directors.

The acting styles of Utpal Dutt's theatre reflect the particular requirements of his theatre. Since in Bengal there are no drama schools that train actors in different styles and traditions, the training of actors happens on the job, as it were, mainly showing what the director wants and is able to train them into. Utpal Dutt's requirements from actors demands fluency of acting idioms and styles. They range from the heroic of the old historical school to the simple imitative acting for a representation of everyday reality, to comic styles. These three styles - natural, heroic-tragic, and comic - have been common in both theatre and films of Bengal. "Character acting," which requires empathy in the actor for his role in producing empathy in the audience is much emphasized. Notions such as alienation-effect (A-effect) of Brecht are not of any importance. Only the comic actor, as in the comedy tradition in general, retains a distance, a critical view of his role. For stylistic resources Dutt turns his attention to jatra conventions and styles for his historical plays involving loud, bold projection and nonnaturalist acting, as well as the training of Shakespeare acting he received early in life in the school of Kendal and experiences of having attended the performances in England of Lawrence Olivier, Paul Schoffield, and others.

The retention of melodrama-based old-stage acting in Utpal Dutt's theatre is particularly useful to his epic-mythic mode, where the hero and the villain are established with a great moral clarity. The acting idiom, including the famous laughter of the villain, is used for presenting us with a moral/political schema which is integral to the heroic mode, as for instance are the idioms of light and music. When the hero Shardul Singh appears in the deck of the rebel ship Khyber, singled out by a spotlight, calling out his refusal to surrender, he functions in the significational frame of Kallol in the same way as the communist flag does at the beginning of the play - flying red and resplendent in the bright light of the "spot." It is interesting to note that Utpal refers far more frequently and reverentially on Stanislavsky's apolitical theatre and theories in the matter of justifying his acting style, than the political stylistics of Brecht or Piscator. His actors are required to lose themselves in the part, no matter how heroic, and hold no sense of irony towards them. Not Brecht's *Mother Courage,* but Utpal Dutt's version of Wagnerian heroes, with their nation-building, or the feudalized jatra/history play's heroic or villainous type characters, become the actor's source of elulation.

From his own account in TART and *Stanislavsky Path* Utpal Dutt's actor-training programme comes out as highly authoritarian and encourages little or no individual initiative or criticality among members of the group. He justifies this by referring to the acting theories of Stanislavsky. In Utpal's hands Stanislavsky's idea of submitting to the "ruling idea" of the text and the role transforms into an absolute submission to the director's dictates. Stanislavsky's training of "psycho-technique" for Utpal translates out into an imperative for breaking the actor's ego and developing an obedience and continuous readiness to submit to the director's needs, rather than the internalization of the part and the personalized projection of it. The mainly liberating aspect of his training programme consists of his demand that his actors become free from religion and politically and historically informed about India, though this is also partially undercut by his attempts to "civilize" the actor by familiarizing hin or her with European literature, music, etc. An acquaintance with Mozart and Beethoven, for example, is considered by him to be the hallmark of an actor's necessary personal development.

Utpal Dutt's eclectic theatre puzzles us at its face value and if we look into his work for what Brecht or Piscator would have called a proletarian or a full-scale or anti-imperialist theatre. But as we have found by examining his political intentions and theatre forms, his eclecticism, which is operative both in the area of content and form, politics and art, leads him into contradictory dimensions. We can simultaneously see both a fit and a gap between these elements of his theatre. On the one hand we have a theatre surface, in the action and the message of the text, where the direct and intended politics of class struggle fight with the form of presentation. Where, instead of mediating each other, the content or intention and representation contradict. On the other hand there is a level which they create by working together. Together they constitute a final political text with a deeper coherence by means of a political and aesthetic symbiosis and reproduces the unclarity of the Stalinist political position itself, with a distinct weight on the bourgeois nationalist component. These different levels of Utpal's theatre have served to confuse critics, who usually argue solely about the surface of the text. The fact that Utpal's contradiction is accounted for by the framework of a national bourgeois socialism is thus invisible to them. Though his intention was to complete an unfinished revolution, which of necessity had to have a national dimension vis-a-vis foreign capital and internally one of class, his political and aesthetic framework precipitated him into contradictions and ambiguities. Nationalism and anti-imperialism become confused and bourgeois social relations are simultaneously questioned and affirmed.

Some of the basic reasons for the class and political character of Utpal Dutt's ambitious project of epic-mythic realism can be summed up in the following points. They follow from the same confusion that IPTA and the communist movement in India as a whole suffers from, namely that of a communism which actively seeks to combine itself with a bourgeois component. From the point of view of constructing a political culture (or theatre) the most explicit factors are that:

a) he maintains a separation between class and culture;

b) he subscribes to a reflectionist view of culture and ultimately in instrumental relationship between culture and politics, thus also seeing culture in terms of discrete products rather than social processes;

c) he equates national theatre and culture primarily with bourgeois or embourgeoisified popular culture and used bourgeois theatre as the vehicle for political theatre;

d) he subscribes to a two-stage theory of socialist revolution (which is deeply embedded in India's communist movement from its first phases) in spite of his and the CPI(M)'s profession to the contrary;

e) for him, as for the communist movement in general, proletarian leadership means the leadership of the primarily middle class led and organized Communist Party.

For these same reasons various bourgeois cultural projects are unproblematic for Utpal. He finds acceptable, for example, Wagner's use of the concept of "the folk" without class connotation, as though all of German society was a homogeneous community. From the Bengali tradition, Girish Gosh's nationalism and Madhushudan's liberal humanism are also attractive for him. He hopes to expand the framework of the professional stage by injecting into it the category "people." He discovers in nationalist playwrights a revolutionary populism, which he outlines in his extensive book on Girish Gosh, Girish Manash. In his plays on the progressive intelligentsia of the nineteenth century, we see that a marginal, radical liberal segment of the middle class, together with their lumpenized peers from the stage, are considered as popular revolutionary forces and classes. Utpal Dutt can reconcile the Hindu nationalist politics of Girish Gosh with the secular liberalism of Madhushudan. Nor does he, in search of a socially binding form, image or myth, ask himself whether or not this harmonious manifestation of the so-called social/cultural unconsciousness depends for its harmony on the imposition on the people of the cultural productions of the ruling and propertied classes. Until one places Utpal's communism in its own tradition of bourgeois enlightenment and liberal progressivism, his astounding concept for both the actual proletariat and the petty bourgeois seem puzzling. We unavoidably come to the conclusion that, given the "cretinous" state of the proletariat, our political and aesthetic resource lies solely in the aesthetics of the bourgeoisie.

It is ironic that all the things Utpal Dutt supposedly wants to resist politically, from cultural imperialism to elitism, become the logical features of his own theatre theories and practices as a result of his secure belonging to a colonial middle class and its particular type of socialism. In terms of his embourgeoisified values and tastes we need to only remind ourselves of the continuous praise and normalization of the European bourgeoisie and their art. The praise of Wagner and claims of affinity with him over the work of Brecht for example, infused Utpal Dutt's own work with a deeply imperialist element. This becomes grossly evident as colonial bourgeois snobbery when he outlines his expectations from his actors and his notion of what it means to be a "cultured" person.

In his discussion about the petty bourgeois actor's shortcomings he lists predominantly, and on par with their lack of information about Indian politics, their lack of knowledge of European literature and culture, their poor English and lack of high Bengali pronunciation. In *Daraon Pathikbar* there is a real fetishization of Madhushudan's Britishism, his knowledge of European classical and romantic literature and languages with which he outsmarts the Europeans. The avid use of little French phrases, or Latin proverbs, does not do much to convince us of the supposed anticolonialist politics embodied in the character nor the frequent laughter raised at the incorrect English of the babus. What is made fun of is not that they need to speak English, but that they do it badly. Madhushudan and his friends however are perfect Black British, and Madhushudan is even more than that in being the first Bengali renaissance man. Madhushudan's proficiency in European literature and language has a peculiar comprador and bourgeois twist, in the snobbery of display of familiarity with things European which are only names to most lower middle-class people. Utpal Dutt's own writing is replete with the same ostentation of erudition - of untranslated quotes or phrases in German and French. These habits are not only redundant, but particularly offensive from somebody whose politics is intended to promote a "national culture" and a socialist revolution. When persued thus culture and colonial/imperialist bourgeois culture become synonymous.

Further affirmation of Utpal Dutts' bourgeois affinities lies not only in the song of praise to the Europeans and a handful of Bengali intellectuals, but also in the patronage and condescension that he shows to "the people" when speaking of peasants and other lower classes. In attempting to justify the anti-intellectual, anticritical and feeling-orientation of his theatre he takes recourse to the excuse that "the people" are passionate and uncritical and thus unable to llike critical/intellectual theatre. They embody for Utpal the collective unconscious of society at its most promitive. According to him they can accept violence, insanity and grand rash emotions because unlike the middle class they are still close to their instincts. This action of "the people" as the other of the rational intellectual contains in it a kind of primitivism that with very little effort can become a part of a fascist ideological apparatus. It is in keeping with Utpal's admiration for Wagner and his use of the concept of "the folk" for a purpose that Utpal considers to be revolutionary.

In the perspective of this cultural politics we can see how the conventions of bourgeois theatre, its commonsense practices, both express and mould Utpal's politics. For Utpal to question these representational modes and apparatuses would be tantamount to questioning the validity of theatre itself as an activity. This is the message in his defensive attacks against those who dare to experiment with and question them This formal conservatism is further facilitated by the fact that Utpal Dutt has an insider's, i.e. a professional's attachment to the bourgeois theatre. This practitioner's knowhow, of being able to produce effects with ready-made devices, is "natural," to him and he is delighted to increase his theatre repertoire. he advances therefore his theory of epic and total theatre which allows him to mix and maximize all aspects of a high technique, high cost and full theatre. A complete formal arsenal is drawn upon for creating "the world-historical," the intended mythic-epic.

This issue of aesthetic representation is more than a question of exterior mechanism of theatre. Lukacs, in the debate on realism, points out the political stake of forms and styles. When he fights for the "realism" of certain representational modes and conventions, he is arguing for the validity of a version of reality and a politics based on that. the conceptual and formal conventions of any work of art direct us towards particular epistemologies and politics. The politics of Utpal's "mythic realism" can not be understood apart from a fuller discussion of this context.

For Utpal Dutt, as for Gorky, myth means a fictional construct on an imaginative abstraction of the essential reality. therefore a myth is not a lie, nor a piece of fantasy. "Myth" signifies the creation of what is "true" by using the imagination to get at the truth, rather than logical reasoning. It is the total result of the "epic" process, which confers a lasting significance to the imaginative discovery by framing, elevating, and enlarging it. The "epic" in this sense is not an oral accretional development through time - as with the ancient Indian epics - but individually existing mythic content. Unlike the traditional epics whose ideological and social purpose remains general and unstated, this epic attempt is directed towards a particular and ideologically formulated political agenda. As Utpal states in *Towards a Revolutionary Theatre,* his mythic project has the ambition of demonstrating in symbolic and fictional form a dialectical and revolutionary view of the world which teaches us the "truth" about reality which must be distinguished from a "fact." Getting at this truth requires getting behind what exists in our everyday life, leaving behind the phenomenal.

If Utpal had stopped at this point he would have been a simple idealist with a matching aesthetic of symbolic realism. But his being a socialist/communist makes the issue more complicated. Though he avoids what he calls the bourgeois vice of empiricism and advocates the use of intuition, he does not want to be seen as an idealist. He feels that as an objective communist who believes in history that he can not advocate "truth" in any universal sense or accomodate a subjectivist view of class and society. He therefore advances the notion of a universal yet essential and objective socialist truth as "class truth" which is arrived at by using intuition and imagination to penetrate into the essential nature of an objective reality which is historical.

Yet, this assurance of objectivity and reference to history, and using the word "class" as an adjective to "truth" does not help Utpal to escape the pitfalls of an objective idealism. It is similar though far less refined to the ideological formulation of Lukacs et al, and appeals to the "laws" of history as objective essences with their internal laws of causality which regulate historical changes. It is still an idealist position, and not the "socio-scientific" method of Brecht for example, where the talk of "laws" are discarded in favour of the social relations. Utpal's mythic worldview can not accomodate experience, observation, comparison, historicization or criticism. For Brecht class is visible at the surface of daily life in the daily social relations. The abstract dialectical "laws" of history with their economic core do not substitute for the uncountable social interactions between people. In Utpal's case however, "class truth" is discovered by a reverse process, by referring back to the "law" of class struggle until the proletariat triumphs. Thus class becomes a settled issue, a given. There is a strong imperative in this position not to attend to the existing social relations in the name of essentiality - the mythic or the quintessential. This "law" of class struggle - as an uncluttered ideological category - forms the core of the mythic, and the epic form provides its expressiive, more-than-life-size form. This is stated quite explicitly by Utpal Dutt when instead of locating any specific action in the existing social organization, he wants the liberty to expunge what actually happens in favour of the historical laws of class struggle.

When we search in Utpal's theatre and theatre criticism for the content of "class truth," we come up again with a notion of class as an objective category with a reflectionist notion of culture. Class can be ascertained in terms of occupation and ownership. To this straightforward economic notion of class is added the notion of an invariant historical law which exists objectively as an inherent principle of dynamism. This provides the basis on which the typicality of action and characterization of the play are structured. For any play to create myth, the degree of idealization and the resulting typicality must be high. This creates a problem by setting up a tension between the scheme of ideal action and typical characters and the semblance of daily life which fills out the play and provides a point of reference for the audience. This subordination of the social, the practical and the experiential to the ideal and the typical makes for great difficulties in constructing plays about actual class and class struggle.

We will examine some of the actual devices through which the mythic realism of Utpal Dutt represents class struggle. As we saw in the section on form, when mythic-realism has to be dramatized Utpal Dutt takes recourse to conventions of Bengali bourgeois theatre and a melodramatic version of Shakespeare. This version of Shakespeare, typified by the tradition of Henry Irving, reworked by directors such as Geoffrey Kendal, with its blend of melodrama and a maximum use of new stage technology, is his main source of inspiration. Discussed by Utpal in connection with Alamgir, it is a kind of speeded-up Elizabethan-Aristotelian structure, with emotional ups and downs, a plot and multiple subplots, which however, hangs together by heroic and villainous actions of a few characters. The plenitude of emotions and incidents of such plays, their sheer quality, are supposed to represent an artistic version of the complexity of social reality. This is in keeping with the Aristotelian (or Elizabethan) bourgeois tradition in which reality must be represented as so many stories rather than as problems. In this dramatic or narrative convention the dramatist must have a complete story to tell, and the text as a whole is conceived as an interweaving of stories which all enrich one central story. Reality, when represented in this mode, is not relational or organizational, but rather a closed unit of a story with a beginning, middle and an end.

This type of closed narrative or dramatic construction that Utpal uses to create a self-contained mythic structure has been resisted from the early part of this century. A look at the debate on realism conducted among Ernst Bloch, George Lukacs and Bertolt Brecht as outlined in *Aesthetic Politics* (ed. F Jameson), shows Block and Brecht's objections to this type of representational form. Their criticism of Lukacs helps throw light on the general problem created by the use of Aristotelian and neoclassical forms by communist realists. According to Brecht, the display of social reality as a "totality" betrays the nature of social reality, which for him is relational and not "total" or apprehensible as such from any locational vantage point. For the purpose of artistic representation which aims for an actual intervention rather than a neat interpretive construction, Brecht devised the edpisodic cum narrative form of epic theatre. He chose from the whole array of expressionist methods, a dramatic equivalent of the technique of montage, that is, a set of episodes that are juxtaposed or joined by a narrative, commenting and choric voices. This not only provoked the audience to work out the textual puzzle, but also actually represented in formal terms the notion of class as social relations and surfaces, rather than self-contained prescribed essences that can be contained in fully rounded "mythic" forms. This continuously interrupoted, continuously relating, juxtaposing form of Brecht's epic theatre challenged both the content and the forms of bourgeois society. Brecht's theatre began and ended in the middle so as to leave the plays as open-ended as possible, because the resolution of the episodic actions does not belong inside but outside of the theatre - in the political arena of society. For him the point of theatre was not to create myths but to demythologize.

Utpal Dutt's dramatic structure in general, and epic-mythic project in particular, contains all the representational devices that Brecht and recent playwrights such as Augusto Boal, for instance, find conservative and repressive. He has a causally organized "plot," with a fully rounded story with its accomplished action; he obeys the unities at times loosely. The multiplicity of emotions and incidents are marshalled to a certain interpretation which is to be taken as the "truth" about history. The action of the play demonstrates laws that work inwardly and inherently in history with their objective causality. There are no loose ends, no pieces. This accounts for the non-interrupted, non-interventionist structure of his plays, where the main theatrical device is dialogue. Therefore a chorus, or a commentator, though sometimes used for formal richness, is not necessary. Where attempts are made at all to go beyond linearity, seriality and causality, to rework space-time relations or show a state of mind (for example in *Sushapner Nagari,* where Utpal uses poor poetry), it jars dreadfully with the rest of the play. It is the same in Tiner Talwar, with a fully conventional sequence of time, place, action and dialogue, where a few moments of fantasy are introduced to project the inner conflict of the director Benimadhab regarding the purpose of theatre. In fully linear plays, the jarring note of introduction of nonlinear conventions merely serves to highlight the conventional, i.e. bourgeois, aspect of Utpal Dutt's theatre, as for example in the two above plays with psychologism and vision.

The hero of Utpal Dutt's epic mythic theatre not so distantly related to the superman. The movement of the action is utterly dependent on special individuals. This becomes apparent in many ways. In plays such as *Stalin 34*, *Tota*, *Daraon Pathikbar*, *Ajeya Vietnam*, and others, the heroic stature of the protagonists is created not only through their own heroic actions, suffering, etc., but by creating a contrasting set - the ordinary people - whose adoration of these characters gives us a signal of how to view them. The protagonosts are idealized and idolized simultaneously. This idolization is in keeping with the Aristotelian conventions of a glorious flaw (hamartia) - a flaw that even a hero may have - or he may even be completely flawless, as in the case of Stalin in the play of the same name. We are prompted to believe that dramatizing "class truth" very nearly amounts to creating an action-packed story of extraordinary individuals who create through passionate and moral confrontations.

The characters in Utpal's plays are "essential" - i.e., "typical" representations. Thereby it is assumed that classes have fixed, objective essences which manifest as character traits in ideal or typical individuals. The character traits always pertain to the laws of class conflicts. For this reason working class, peasant, middle class and military heroes are hard to differentiate and share the same characteristics. Stalin and the nineteenth-century peasant leader Titumir have essentially the same dialogue in the same language of heroism, courage and self-sacrifice. They speak as should all leaders of the people. Even the ruling class heroic figures transcend the interests and politics of their class and identify themselves with those below them, for a national cause. The heroes rising from within the lower classes, on the other hand, are some sort of "nature's aristocrats" or born leaders. The politics of mythic-epic is one of following the leader, who however does not need to understand history but embodies its principle. This mythic heroic figure is marked by vast, sweeping passions commensurable to the status of a spirit of an age or class. These feelings are suitably displayed through patriotism and heroism in battles (*Tota*), through patriotism, poetry and excessive temperament (*Stalin Pathikbar*), or dedication to socialist revolution (*Stalin 1934* or *Ajeya Vietnam*). Empathy and admiration for a hero or a leader figure - both within and outside of the text - are the staples of Utpal's epic project. Feeling, not criticality, is here assumed as the agent of change, both for the characters and the audience.

This appeal to vast feelings or passions is meant to enliven the otherwise dull and abstract notion of the type, and escite the audience into anger against tyranny. Utpal is insistent on the claim that all theatre, by which he means European and Indian, from Shakespeare to Ibsen or Gorky, is a grand attempt to create deep feelings in the audience. He indulges in frequent invectives and denunciations against the Bengali middle classes, particularly the poor sectors, for their lack of passion. He thinks that the ability to feel has shrunk among the petty-bourgeois, thus deadening heroic impulses. This is the very "cul-de-sac" of the petty-bourgeois life that he speaks of. In his eyes the emotions to be found among his middle-class audience and actors provide no ground for political theatre.

On the other hand, he tells us that "the people" of Bengal, the peasantry, do not suffer from the atrophy of feelings that characterizes the middle classes. This is his view of the people or the "folk," as the primitive. "The people" inhabit the world of the "folk," or legends, of religious superstition and do not understand the restrictive standards of rationality, criticism and science. They are solely emotional. Utpal Dutt justifies the excessive emotionalism of his plays by saying that "political theatre has to stand in front of those little or half-educated audiences who don't dissect madness [of Hamlet or Ophelia] under a bourgeois microscope" (Dutt, 1977, p. 13). Providing them with feelings rather than criticality is the only way to politically educate them. "We will have to take theatre to those who are sunk in the tradition of *Ramayana* and *Mahabharata*" (Dutt, 1977, p. 13). This sort of statement reads strangely in view of the fact that Utpal Dutt and the PLT actually perform the bulk of their shows through the year to petty-bourgeois middle-class audiences. "The people" and their imputed theatre habits seem to be more than justification for Utpal's own theatre habits and needs.

The excessiveness of feelings to which the members of Utpal's audience are encouraged through his theatre is supposed to testify to their political involvement. The collective political impact of a play is measured on the strength of feelings that it is able to evoke in the audience. Though Utpal Dutt claims an affinity between his theatre and the "total" and epic theatre of Irwin Piscator, with his stage of hundreds and all available productive forces, it is difficult not to point out that Piscator was critical, unheroic, and severe - and not a member of the cult of feelings. The stage animator of *The Good Soldier Schweik,* the teacher of Peter Weiss and Ralph Hochhuth, Piscator would have despised Utpal's glowing outbursts of patriotism, nationalism, and folkism. It is interesting that in spite of the objectivity and economism of Utpal's concept of class, his ultimate reliance for political results of theatre is on something so subjective. It seems as though it is the motor of feelings rather than political organizations based on class that moves history. The objective laws and class essences can not otherwise have any dynamism which can be transformed into theatre. the politics of Utpal Dutt's theatre feeling is finally attached to an idealist, petty-bourgeois morality which is activated by the way the story of class struggle is told. As Max Raphael put it in *Proudhon, Marx, Picasso,* the petty-bourgeois revolutionary work of art stand as the mediating conscience between science and politics. In the idealized scheme of class struggle, even when a story begins on the social terrain an abstract and idealist formulation necessary for the mythic quickly moves it from the realm of the political to that of the moral and the emotional - where the social and organizational specificity of the situation is expunged in favour of constructing an allegory of good fighting evil. Each history play thus loses its historicity and becomes an extended allegory, each political story a moral tale.

The type of realism then that emerges from this mythopoeic aesthetic is allegorical and iconic. The types that are deduced from the ideal laws of social dialectic are really more like icons of class, rather than the individuals or characters in the bourgeois tradition. If anything they smack of feudalism, of medieval morality plays, where in the name of Shakespearean absolute and ideal moral categories (good or bad angel, mercy, seven deadly sins, etc.) they wrestled over the soul of Everyman as in *Dushapner Nagari*. The enactment of ideal action performed by idealized subjects or agents, imbued by moral conflicts, together form the core of Utpal Dutt's mythic-epic theatre. This idealized political scheme, which does not really leave much for the audience to do except to feel the right passions and adore the right hero and the leader, and follow him on his historical mission, is hardly the theatre which can stimulate and mobilize towards an active and popular class strugle. The bourgeois national element, both in content and form, and political intent, overdetermine class struggle. Utpal Dutt's eclectic and mainly bourgeois theatre, guided by socialist realism and revolutionary romanticism, parallels his eclectic and contradictory politics. Here we have a whole different range of politics within the parameter of bourgeois nationalism.

Ultimately we must remember that Utpal Dutt's purpose is to create myth by using an epic mode, as opposed to subjecting myths to the scrutiny of the epic form. We must also remember that he inherited this project of socialist myth-building from the tradition of socialist realism. It so happens that the Soviet agenda also sought to bring together socialism, patriotism and nationalism. And this could not be done by means of critical realism. In the Soviet Union, having a socialist government in place, bourgeois society and class struggle were considered things of the past, and certainly divisive in a situation where divisions existed not only between the left and the right but also among the ranks of the left itself. Soviet cultural policy from the mid-1920s onwards is fraught with stronger and stronger directives to the writers to engage in the project of nation-building, as well as to diffuse possibilities of class struggle at levels other than those which are explicitly economic and political. From *Kollontai* to proletcult, from Mayakovsky to Eisenstein, all were prevented from asking disturbing and divisive questions. What was required - and even Gorky tired of this after a short enthusiastic period - were forms which would be acceptable to bourgeois or semifeudal tastes and distinctly carry on in a continuous tradition, but which would be instrumentally used to popularize a socialist economy and its state. The work of the myth-maker was to leave behind the grimy, sordid, immediate and the experiential - particularly at a social level - and project the view of a classless society, an ideal class struggle. The utopianism of this cultural enterprise, needless to say, actually leaves intact bourgeois social formations. Class struggle takes place primarily at the level of economic and political power. The conscious myth-building with a worker hero - whose visual equivalents are in the many communist posters of the era - becomes a normative fantasy. Though it is supposed to serve as an encouragement for "the people," it can become a distant and unconnected image, if not at times a condemnation of what actually people are at any given point in time. It certainly does not tell one how to get to the ideal stage from the present one.

What seems to have been forgotten in this attempt to consciously create a national literature of socialism, both in India and the Soviet Union, is the fact that myths, even of proletarian revolution, can not be created by an individual choice, either by a limited number of persons or even by a successful communist party. Even while disputing the notions of collective unconscious and primal archetypes as the ground for myth - it is easily admissible that myths hold in suspension a common but contradictory set of practices and beliefs of large numbers of people over a long period of time and are not consciously advanced ideological tasks. Myths are not created for the purpose of creating myths, they develop out of existing stories. They are a combination of existing narratives, images, experiences and emotions - polyvalent significations - that have a patina of time and long use on them. Myths in that context are not meant to be inflated artistic generalizations but highly nuanced particularities. To hide the specificity of the mundane and the everyday was never the purpose of myth, but to crystalize them in a revealing manner. Conscious mythic projects are at best redundant, at worst, due to the formal and epistemological compromises that have political implications, pernicious to the cause of class struggle. A myth-building exercise is an ideological exercise and not a substitute for, or to be confused with, the culture of resistance which is thrown up in a popular process of class struggle, where myths happen. An artist can only produce his or her art, it becomes a myth by being inserted into a popular social and political process. If we keep this in mind then we can see how - for all of the reasons outlined so far - India's incomplete revolution could not be completed through such cultural projects as that of Utpal Dutt. His scheme of mythic realism is an aesthetic manifestation of his nationalist bourgeois socialism.

REFERENCES

Theatre Bulletin. Calcutta, May-June 1980.
Bharucha, Rustam. *Rehearsals of Revolution.* Honolulu: University of Hawaii Press, 1983.
Dutt, Utpal. *Tiner Talwar.* Calcutta: Jatiya Shahitya Parishad, 1973.
_________. *Stanislavskir Path.* Calcutta: Epic Prakashani, 1976.
_________. *Epic Theatre.* Calcutta, 1977.
_________. *Chaer Dhoan.* Calcutta: Jatiya Shahitya Parishad, 1979.
_________. *Towards a Revolutionary Theatre.* Calcutta: M C Sarkar, 1982.
_________. *Stanislavsky Theke Brecht.* Calcutta: Natya Bhabana, 1982a.
_________. *Japenda Japenja.* Calcutta: Natya Bhabana, 1984.
Franklin, Bruce (ed.). *The Essential Stalin.* Garden City, NJ: Anchor Books, 1972.
Gorky, Maxim. *Collected Works,* vol 10. Translated by Igor Kruvtsov. Moscow: Progress Publishers, 1978-82.

One Woman, Two Women, Without Women: Gender Construction in Bengali Theatre

A curious title? But it can be explained. If one were to thumb through the pages of Bengali theatre magazines (and these magazines are the expressions of progressive/alternative/left theatre producers, critics and theatre-lovers), one would come across these curious lines. They would be found in the ads announcing the publications of new, often revolutionary plays. They are an appeal to theatre groups who buy the plays, to consider staging them, so they would not be put through the difficult task of finding women for the cast.

The groups, it should be clear from this, are mostly male - with a few women dotting their compositions - therefore "one woman, two women, without women" is the safety code, the no risk sign. For me, these innocuous words epitomize both the history and the current status of women in Bengali theatre, its gendered construction, the social situation and availability of actresses, the duration of their acting careers, their roles, their economic security, their artistic independence and strength.

Without Women: A History of Women in Theatre in Bengal

Public theatre in Bengal from its beginnings in 1873, like theatre elsewhere, has been a man's world. Wherever performing activities lost their ritual character and became "entertainment," and where society split into private and public spheres, theatre has been considered a "public" domain. This and the fact of patriarchy - which relegates women to the status of property and producers of heirs (male) - has assigned women, in spite of their hard labour in fields and elsewhere, to the private sphere as their proper domain. The more "civilized" the society (i.e. private property, surplus exploitation and class-based societies), the more the "interiorization" or "privatization" of women. "Good" women (wives, mothers, daughters and sisters) have paid for their "good"ness by complete subordination, illiteracy and absence from the public sphere in decisive roles.

And so, it is not without reason that those women who fell from (or left) that enclosed sphere were and are designated as "public" women. In fact, in

Bengali the euphemism for prostitute is "Bajarer Meyechhele" - a "market woman." Women in general, however, were protected from becoming "bad" or going "public." Furthermore it was feared that their presence, if not always actively corrupting, would at least create problems in the theatre world. Until recently, and even now in the Bengali countryside's indigenous theatre form called jatra, men still play women's parts. In the first phase of Bengali public theatre, "good" women not only didn't act, they didn't even feature as audience. As long as theatre was staged in the private homes of wealthy landlords and urban businessmen, women were allowed to see the performance, though from within a special corner secluded with bamboo slats, where they could see without being seen, while their menfolk, dressed as women, acted their parts. But when in 1873, in imitation of English "hall" staging, regular professional public theatre developed among the Bengalis, it caused "good" women to lose access even as audience.

A new rich class - their taste developed by their exposure to and acceptance of British culture - were the chief patrons of the professional stage, although the bulk of the attendance was provided by a rising middle class, known as "babus" (gentlemen). "Babus" were white-collar workers, involved in servicing and managing British business and the state. The women who frequented the theatre with the "babus" were not "good." Since much of the white-collar sector lived without their families, who remained in their "country homes," a thriving trade in prostitution had developed. And there was prestige attributed to being able to keep many, or particularly well-known, prostitutes. "Womanizing" habits of the rich and the babus gave rise to a plethora of satires and farces, along with other Western habits of "free-living" and "free love" - reflecting the fact that that urban living in colonial India had thrown overboard many habits and customs of a more prohibitive, community-oriented society.

But speaking of the bibis (gracious ladies), rather than the babus, Calcutta had become well stocked with women whose living depended on prostitution. They came from impoverished peasant background (there was not yet any significant working class) and quite often from the genteel life of higher castes. They were there because they had "fallen." In a country where marriages were arranged for women as young as eight or ten years of age, with husbands often much older, and where among high class brahmins (Kulins) polygamy was permitted, widows were an all-pervasive presence and easy victims of male seduction. Socially unacceptable and rejected by their families, often with no means of support, one thing led to another, and many of these "fallen" women found themselves in the blind alleys of the prostitute quarters.

Necessity or, perhaps, an attempt to improve their fees and class, led many of these women to take up "entertainment" as part of their routine. This sometimes minimized the number of tricks necessary, as well as fetching clients who came for the entertainment. An excellent performer might develop a "patron," her own babu, who would keep her or even take her to a private house, often to his Garden House (Bagan Bari). It is to be noted that it was at this time, at the height of a social turnover, and in a city filled with the vices of a parasitic petty bourgeoisie, that Iswar Chandra Vidya Sagar, a noted educationist, launched his campaign for widow remarriage - a disturbing, unheard-of practice.

However depressing the life of a prostitute was, it was here that some women developed performing skills to an astonishing degree. The days of education had not yet arrived for women; nor, when they came, did they unfetter "good" women to take part in the entertainment world's public life. In the world of theatre frequented by men whose hobby and passion this art was, there was too much respectability and concern for public morality to bring in women right away. But, in time, there emerged in the theatre world a group of educated men who had moved away from this petty bourgeois respectability and had overcome the hierarchical habits of caste. They were a sort of social rebel and they, combined with the young rebellious intelligentsia with whom their values often converged, represented a shift in social norms. They had no objection to trying women out for "female" roles. In this context, Michael Madhusudan Dutta, a young playwright and poet of extraordinary power and strong anti-imperialist politics, played a major role in introducing actresses to the theatre world. In 1873, the Bengali "national theatre" decided to accept women and put on a play by Michael called Sarmishtha, an antibrahminical, antihierarchical play which reinterpreted an episode from the Hindu epic Mahabharata. Four women were found among the demi-monde circles who displayed extraordinary histrionic ability. The tradition of prostitute-entertainers, by this means, finally shifted to new ground - the private world of entertainment was joined to the public world of theatre.

Gradually, women became a standard feature of this public world and, if they were excellent, received wide acclaim and a degree of respectability. But it still didn't make them "good" - i.e. marriageable - women. Ironically, however, they often played "chaste" wives and virgins, singing praises of the values which victimized them, or the roles of boys, young men, gods (e.g. Krishna) and saints, where great delicacy was required of both person and voice.

The presence of women on the stage in major roles and their high artistic and commercial appeal would argue that these actresses had some power behind the scenes as well. But this was hardly the case. Women who came onto the stage were socially and economically powerless and dependent, for the length of their artistic careers. After all, there was a great abundance of "fallen" women from amongst whom the director-lead actors could choose. Women were only poorly paid actresses, often owned by their patron babu who, with the director, decided the artistic and economic life of these women.

The case of Binodini, a veritable empress of the stage, is worth some notice. Highly versatile as an actress, and accomplished in music and dance, beautiful in her person, seeking education and artistic fulfillment, Binodini wished to retire from the stage at the age of twenty-three. Her body and mind were put up for sale by her mentor, the great actor-director Girish Chandra Ghosh. He persuaded her in favour of a patron who, in lieu of a cash offer, promised to build a "hall" for her. Binodini's artistic soul acquiesced to this because, above all, she was an actress, a theatre person; when the hall was being constructed she carried mortar with the labourers, such was her enthusiasm.

Her mentor and fellow actors had promised that the hall would be named after her as "B Theatre." But when the time of registration came, the hall was called "Star Theatre" and the registration was in the name of four favourite male actors of Girish Ghosh. Binodini, who could have accepted a vast sum of money instead of the theatre, now had neither.

The patron eventually ceased to be interested in her, and her old lover was gone. For a while she continued to perform on this same stage, until she noticed that other women were replacing her in Girish Ghosh's attention and training. Finding another babu patron, Binodini retired forever from the stage, but the semi-wife status that she enjoyed came to an end when this patron died - his family, of course, never accorded any proper social status to her.

The life of this woman - who was by all contemporary accounts the most acclaimed actress of her time - as narrated in her autobiography *Amarkatha* (My Story), is an object lesson on the problem of women in the theatre world. No matter what she did, squeezed in between the devil of the male-dominated stage and the deep sea of male-dominated society, she had no power to carry on her artistic career or any other independent one.

The great actresses, then as now, are not owners or directors of theatre companies. The Binodinis of this world could never legitimize aspirations to become theatre businesswomen in their own right. They seemed, actually, to have retained and often nurtured many of the self-effacing sacrificing traits of their "good" counterparts - undoubtedly out of necessity. Not the least of these traits was referred to as the "eternal urge" (to quote one male historian) to build a "nest" and to be accorded "the proper maternal status" - the role of a "constant, chaste wife." Even great actresses such as Binodini seemed to fall into the "good woman" syndrome. The parts they played on stage, historical-mythological, chaste-heroic mothers, daughters and wives, or seductresses (ultimately cut down by the punishing arm of fate) seem proper adjuncts to these dreams of respectability.

Great as they were in talent, these women never defined their own roles, or played any part that related positively to their lives. Choreographed and coached in acting by male directors, who often wrote the plays and played the male leads, star actresses such as Golap (Rose), Binodini (the pleasing one) and Tara Sundari (Lovely Star), were more like highly sensitive reflectors in which men viewed their own fantasies.

Even now, nearly one hundred years later, Binodini has given rise to a lot of males theatrical fantasies, supposedly sympathetic. But these plays always mourn her violated love life, trust and dreams - never the death of the artist or the loss to the stage, at her withdrawal.

One Woman: An Interview with Sova Sen

Since Binodini's time, the theatre world has grown much larger and now, essentially, consists of two quite separate tendencies. First, there are the commercial theatre companies (which are businesses where directors and actors are employees). These are the more direct outgrowth of historical public theatre traditions. This is the business of entertainment.

But there are also "group" theatres; these are "amateur" groups where no one is paid, though they produce regular shows in halls with tickets. Group theatres numerically, as well as culturally, outbid the commercial theatre. This is the world of theatre as "art" and as education. Social and political consciousness-raising, as well as formal experimentation, are on the agenda. This theatre owes its existence to the Indian Peoples Theatre Association (IPTA) which was created by the Indian Communist Party (1943) in order to link theatre with politics. IPTA was eventually fragmented by internal aesthetic and political struggles, which led to the traditions of Gananatya (people's theatre) and Nabanatya (new theatre) - Gananatya leaning very heavily on politics, while Nabanatya more concerned with psychological and formal experimentation. Though rigid distinctions between the two are not always possible, the group theatre movement of today includes both tendencies.

The acting environment of group theatre is quite unlike that which preceeded it. The actors and actresses come from the middle class and, very often, have some kind of left/progressive political stand. In order to understand the position women hold in the theatre, I spoke with Sova Sen, acclaimed as the most dynamic actress in the group theatre movement. Her acting career began with the first notable performance by the IPTA in 1943 and she has remained in the theatre world through thousands of nights of acclaimed performances.

Sova Sen's commitment to political theatre has continued unbroken since 1944, but she is also important for us because she has struggled both on personal and political grounds and emerged triumphant. Her mere presence in the theatre as a woman during the forties, combined with her divorce and the fact that she was already a mother at the time of her second marriage - all these created very great difficulties for her in a society that continues, even to this day, to be semifeudal in many ways. Her contribution to Bengali theatre consists not only of her survival, nor even of her impressive acting talent; she has also built and maintained, with her (playwright-director-actor) husband, Utpal Dutt's two major theatre groups: Little Theatre Group and People's Little Theatre - PLT being the largest and most accomplished of Calcutta's theatres.

We began by talking about the differences in the social perception of actresses between when she entered the stage and now. She said that although things were somewhat better and easier in the group theatre movement now, they were still difficult.

> The major obstacles for women in pursuing their acting careers are some traits in the character of the Bengali middle-class males . . . They may rate these traits as virtues; we women think they are vices. With those attitudes it will be very difficult for women to come out and associate with the outside world of cinema, theatre - with the cultural world at large. I faced these problems myself, except that I had an advantage. I entered the theatre world with a political idealism - I was associated with the IPTA. So wherever we went, we were respected for that. But I have noticed that other actresses, acting on par with me, without those advantages, could not survive the harrassments . . .
>
> Ever since childhood I had an ambition that I would overcome the hazards and obstacles put in women's paths. In doing effective work in the outside world, I felt that I would rise above the distrust that men have towards women and prove that women can remain "good" and yet work outside . . .
>
> And about being "good" or "bad" - who defines what's "good"

anyway?

It helps to come from middle-class homes, be educated and have a political idealism, but it also seems that the image is "cleaner" if these actresses are economically independent of theatre. Many work in offices, schools and colleges or are supported by their families and so are not as vulnerable as those actresses who need to make a living. These financially independent actresses are not socially ostracized for doing theatre.

From the 1920s onwards, more and more middle-class women joined the public life of education and politics. Independence, gained in 1947, further accelerated women's public involvement. In Bengal, for instance, independence produced both physical and economic dislocation through the partition and relocation of the population. Bengali women sought many kinds of employment for survival and perfectly "respectable" women found themselves in many unconventional jobs, including acting. Now, while this naturalized acting to some extent as a decent woman's occupation, a change from which all women reaped benefit, still the women who sought it as an economic career were entering diffficult zones. There is still a stigma attached to their presence on the stage.

On the other hand, Sova Sen also drew my attention to the fact that the respectability of group theatre has its own burdens for women. The family's "normal" expectations of a female member continue unabated. Whereas the older actresses could see this as their major "job" and devote vast amounts of time to the theatre, the new actress's choice is taken far less seriously - both by her and by her family. When she is awarded the honour of wifehood and motherhood, she has less legitimate time for acting - family continues to be her first priority.

> There will always be struggles and hassles in the theatre movement, particularly for women. Take for instance finding women for the parts. We ran Minerva theatre professionally and all through we were bugged by this problem. There are two ways of getting actresses. Some women come with some sort of idealism. Others just to take a chance - if you become a member of Utpal Dutt's group you may get a chance in films. We did get some women who had fought all obstacles to get there, but couldn't carry on for too long. They had to leave because of all kinds of family problems. We got mighty few who could last out.

Since theatre could neither produce nor solve these social problems in itself, Sova Sen located them in the prevailing gender roles in Bengal, which she sees as organized through class structures. At one point, she contrasted the world of property and social respectability of the middle-class women with the conduct of the working-class women:

> Women of the peasantry, of lower classes, don't put up with as much [gender-based] abuse . . . as ours do. They have an economic equality of sorts with their men . . . They earn about equal amounts, working side by side. So if men oppress them - if he hits her - she has the option of hitting back. Because they don't have as much at stake in things like property, dowry, respectability . . . if needs be, they can break up their home and leave. But our middle-class women are torn with doubts and conflicts: what will people think of me if I leave? Who will feed me and my children? Maybe I'll end up in a worse place, etc . . .
> You see feudalism still lives in every cell of our society, particularly among men. They are brought up with such protection and service! A boy doesn't even have to get himself a glass of water. Even among the working class. Always a woman comes back from work and starts her household duties. Everyone accepts this - men and women! It's seen as natural. If a husband enters the kitchen, people are shocked. What! You are cooking? That reality is unthinkable. These attitudes, regressive traits within us - if we can't get rid of these, sweep them clean, nothing can help women.

The subordination of women, the assymetrical social relations which produce such strictly gender-based expectations - these rise from everyday life to the stage and recycle back. From the late nineteenth century to now, the image of the woman, of male-female relations, of family relations, have not changed much in theatre or film. The degree to which women's roles are positive or progressive depends solely on the state of consciousness of the, inevitably, male playwright-director. In fact, even when seemingly progressive (i.e. not overly sadistic or humiliating), the portrayal of women continues to be patriarchal. A heroic mother, a revolutionary companion of a revolutionary man - provided as serious comments on social change - are still constituted by the same stereotypes, sentimentality and feudal traditions of the pulp cinema.

Even when some nontraditional behaviour is acceptable, for instance in *Three Penny Opera* or *The Good Woman Szechaun,* it is because, as Sova Sen put it, "they were Western women." But even productions of Brecht, in the hands of some Bengali playwright-directors, are often transformed from political theatre into Bengali social dramas.

Chetana's production of Brecht's *Mother* (based on the novel by Maxim Gorky, of the same name) is a good example of such misinterpretation. The play attempts to shift the connotation of "mother" to one of nurturing in general, therefore making the word applicable to a people as a whole. As such, by the end of the play, the mother becomes a comrade to her son, and they, along with other Russian revolutionaries, become potential mothers of the revolution. Yet, Chetana intensifies the gender role to its highest degree, producing instead a super-mother - the ultimate Bengali woman of the film-theatre tradition - a woman ready to mother a whole revolution.

Bengali theatre tradition is replete with this myth of all-sacrificing motherhood, while the lover role oscillates between the rhetoric of revolution and the sweet saccharine of "true love." The dialogues, the inflection, the gestures, often make it hard to believe that these plays are produced with the intent of revolutionizing the social unconscious of the Bengali middle class.

"Where," I asked Sova Sen, "do these roles originate from?"

"Partly from life," she replied, "and partly from their fantasies."

"But do middle-class Bengali women ever behave in this way?"

"No, they do put up with a lot, they are forced to; but their struggle is not so visible. After all, how many of them are economically independent? Without that, it's almost impossible to put up a fight . . . She may say many things, but ultimately returns to that bedroom . . . And our playwrights, who are males, are watching us - that most of us will put up with a lot. I think it pleases them because they are men themselves. Men take their wives to plays like *Don't Wipe Away My Vermillion* (i.e. end my marriage). Let the women see this - how patiently they should serve their masters, put up with tortures . . ."

But Sova Sen's roles are different - some quite repugnant to the sensibility of the conservative middle class. She insists that she has never been "type" cast.

> I didn't have to face being "type" cast. Because Utpal was the playwright. He wrote the plays based on his knowledge of me and my acting. He is also the director and an actor; he understands my acting potential better than anyone else, so he shaped the parts according to that.
>
> This role I had in *Kallol* was great. She is a Maharashtrian lady who defies her son to protect her daughter-in-law who's living with someone else. "OK," she says, "so you went away to war, then you didn't think about us. You didn't know or care how we lived . . . now, if your wife is with someone else because she had to live, she can't be blamed for

> that. What gives you the right to turn up now and challenge her?" You know she is also an old lady and she joins hands with the revolutionaries . . .
>
> Now here's a woman who fights her son, to protect another woman (her daughter-in-law). We have to see this as a very big event in our theatre history.

Sova Sen's portrayals of women, both in dialogue and performance, may retain some of the traditional features (for example, the convention of motherhood); but, she rids the characters of their passivity, emphasizing a toughness, a heroism, and introducing active elements of initiative and dynamism. (There are also, quite often, conscious satires on men's expectations of women.) Probably in a conscious tribute to actresses such as Binodini, Utpal Dutt wrote a play *Tiner Talwar* (The Tin Sword) in which Sova Sen plays the part of an actress for whom the stage is the highest priority. Both she and a younger actress scorn marriage and family life in order to live as actresses, as artists. This play, and a few others, bring together the old and the new in a revolutionary reversal of social attitudes. Our conversation, itself, testified to these changing values, by the respect she showed towards actresses who came from the "lower walks of life":

> When I first joined the films, I spent quite a lot of time with these actresses. I received such affection, respect from them, got training and help in acting. Some of them wept when they told me that their children could not enroll in the schools. I was amazed. What crime did these women commit?

She also spoke of the world of jatra (travelling, nonproscenium, village- and town-based theatre), in which actresses are paid, but which is different from both group and commercial theatre:

> . . . great actresses [are] also very well paid. Those who work in the jatrs live in a separate world. How much do they have to to do with your so-called "society"? They wander around seven or eight months a year performing . . . with very little contact with family life. Sometimes they come home - for a night or two - and leave. And among them, both men and women live differently. Some men, who have wives in their village or town, have a different companion within the jatra world. The jatra world has accepted this . . . when women have children, the child is looked after by the actress's mother or sister . . .

> In Calcutta's commercial theatre things are different. This theatre is seen practically as an extension of a sleazy night life, the world of entertainment. Women within this are looked down upon, are not "artists," nor political activists from the safe precincts of the middle-class life. They are workers; as entertainers, they do as they are told. It is here that the old theme of theatres as brothels continues. Actresses have to work as strippers - a play called *Bar Bodhu* (The Prostitute) ran over a few years on the strength of strip scenes.

With her characteristic astuteness, Sova Sen pointed her finger at the economic vulnerability of the women and gave an example of the generalized corruption of theatre as business.

> You must keep this in mind - who runs these shows? Behind each venture there's a huge fat capitalist. Some are into steel or iron, others into something else - all pots of black money. Playwrights produce what these financiers demand. After all, in our country no one can live on writing plays . . . People don't read plays, they see them . . . so then they have to lick the boots of these owners, to make a living.

Sova Sen felt that for any real change, i.e., reorganization of theatre on a nongendered and noncommodity basis, there would have to be fundamental struggles on both class and gender lines. To change relations of inequality was a long-range struggle to which she, as a communist, was partisan. But in the short run, she agreed with my suggestion that there should be an actresses' association or union that would deal with both the problems of economic insecurity and of sexual harassment, so that "when women want to act they don't fall into the clutches of directors and aren't forced to yield." There should be an economic angle too. "Actresses are begging in old age or are burdens on their families - if they have them, that is . . . Actors, actresses and playwrights ought to unite in their struggle, try to solve this problem of making a living, collectively. That might work. Some people are trying to."

Two Women, More Women: Looking to a Future

In what this veteran actress had to say, speaking from the trenches of cultural and political struggles, it was apparent that there was great personal strength and, in her example, reason for hope. Yet although a "new woman" now stands on the stage in Bengal, the theatre itself remains structurally the same as the one *not* named for Binodini.

The fundamental changes which are necessary can happen only if and when women own or run their own theatres, write and direct their own plays, and also act in them. And even then, unless the authors are committed to actively challenging the social, political and cultural status quo, the fact of their gender will not in itself be enough to transform the institution. Challenges will undoubtedly emerge from a socialist/communist, as well as feminist, perspective. They must examine and expose the interactions of gender and class; how class is engendered and gender class-ified. Such a movement is beginning with strong women actresses and a couple of women directors who are now emerging.

Madhushri Dutta, a woman graduate of the National School of Drama, has formed a collective of about twenty people - both men and women. Their group, *Anarya* (The non-Aryans), has translated and mounted an ambitious production recently of Bertolt Brecht's *Mother Courage and Her Children*. And Usha Ganguli has produced a play in Hindi called *Maha Bhoj* (The Banquet), for a Bengali- and Hindi-speaking audience. *Maha Bhoj*, a political satire with great dynamism and a cast of about thirty-five people, received a critics' award for best play of the year; and Usha is currently planning a production with a mainly female cast.

Such women, we may hope, mark the beginnings of a movement towards the erasure from Bengali theatre of the "necessity" of advertising plays by the reassuring coda, "One Woman, Two Women, Without Women . . ."

The Alienated Hero in the Novels of Sunil Gangyopadhyay

The alienated, lonely individual has featured as the hero in numerous Bengali novels of the last two decades. I am going to examine some of the characteristics of this hero in the novels of Sunil Gangyopadhyay. He has produced more than twenty novels, which speaks for great popularity with the reading public. This seems to indicate that he somehow manages to reflect or satisfy the social values and expectations of publishers and his readers to a great extent. What these social values are will be the subject of exploration of this essay. In no way will it be an assessment of the formal quality of these novels.

I would like to introduce Sunil's hero in a trivial situation and an awkward posture, where his self-importance and self-consciousness are both displayed at the same moment:

> I got down at Begumpur station for a drink of water. The tube-well was very small and I had to stoop very low in order to catch the water in the cup of my palms. This method of drinking may quench the thirst, but it is not very satisfying. The whole body takes on an awkward, unseemly twist, feet spread apart to avoid the splash. It's a real nuisance! But on a hot summer afternoon thirst is unavoidable.

This is from the first paragraph of the novel *Tumi Ke?* (Who Are You?). It seems as though the hero is looking at a mirror, with almost a matinee idol's awareness of the need to maintain a graceful persona, in which the two elements that are stressed are absolute control and symmetry. Even in an obscure and deserted railway platform he seems to feel on display, and the uncomfortable nature of his situation is heightened when two more characters enter the scene, who "stand right next to me, with a flask and a small cup. But I can't ask for the cup. It is not in my nature to do such things." But there are some people who are not above such things, as we see from the next sequence:

> . . . [a] thin, dried-up-looking man rushed up at a great pace and asked with remarkable ease, "Brother, may I have the cup for a minute?" The owner of the flask replied very affably, "Yes, of course." There is nothing unusual about this. If one person owns a cup another may wish to use it. Especially if he remembers to rinse it before returning. Then things are maintained at a seemly level for all. And yet why could I not ask for it?

The answer is perhaps simple-because he is a unique individual, a hero, and this sort of plebeianism of community-living does not appeal to him. Now, if it is thought that I am reading too much into too little, I must point out that this apparently trivial scene of drinking at the public tap drags on for three pages. It seems reasonable to assume, then, that this was done in order to establish the major characteristic traits of the hero. We too should continue with it a little longer.

While the hero stands by in a stance of polite detachment, the graceless thin man "drank three cups of water in rapid succession," indulged in a satisfied exclamation and "completely ignoring the owners of the glass, said to me graciously, 'You won't be able to manage it like that. Here, take this.' " The hero, though unable to ask for a favour, can, however accept it if it is volunteered. He takes the glass, without bothering to ask for the permission of the owners, who are presumably standing close by. He also notices, with his background of impeccable manners, that "the thin man vanished without much further ado, without troubling to express his gratitude by thanking anybody." It seems immaterial that he himself has not thanked anyone either, or noticed the helpfulness of the thin man. But a poorly dressed person, whose undernourished body is frequently brought to our attention, is obviously not the right object of a gentleman's gratitude. The lack of weight, smoothness and good manners all indicate the inferior social class of this man, whereas the hero, as we learn eventually, works in a high position in an industrial monopoly. He does wash the cup when he returns it.

It is only natural that such a man should resent being mistaken for someone else, especially by people who matter socially. After all, "both the men were wearing faultlessly cut shirts and trousers. Both wore sunglasses, and even the flask they had was very expensive." Undeniably they matter a great deal because they represent class in themselves, and an obstacle - potential competitors - for the hero. As such our hero promptly decides to annihilate them. He decides to forget their names: "I decide to get rid of many unnecessary things in order to keep my memory well ventilated." The offence of the mistaken identity he converts to his own advantage, but not before he makes his displeasure noted. "I don't like this at all. I feel quite angry with this Asit Majumdar. After all everyone needs his own, individual distinctiveness."

By the time the hero returns to the train, his seat has been partially encroached upon. After grumbling a little about the inconvenience of travelling by second or third class he informs us that "nowadays I rarely travel on my own money. My company always pays for first-class fares." He finds it intolerable to rub shoulders with people who are condemned to pay their own fares or travel illegally. Even the women are repulsive to him. "There is no one who can hold my eyes for long. Not even the three young women. In their very looks and manners there is something which reminds one of kitchens and boiled plantains." He is also aware of an intellectual deficiency in them.

> The two men on my either side have been finally discouraged from attempts at conversation with me by my monosyllabic replies. Now they are discussing the Swedish social system. *I can feel* that most of what they are saying is wrong. I too know next to nothing about Sweden, but somehow one can detect quite often from the voice when people are ignorant. [Italics mine]

It is possible to argue with rational judgements of ordinary mortals, but what can one advance against the infallible intuition of the distinctive individual?

He leaves this unbearable company and paces about on the platform, carefully avoiding the people who, out of vulgar curiosity, want to know the reason for the train's delay. His eyes are fixed on the window of the first-class compartment, where faces have gathered to watch him. This attention, while flattering, leaves something to be desired. "I felt like telling the whole world to look at me for myself." And there, next to the window of the air-conditioned compartment, sits his ideal of femininity "in a dark red sari, matching blouse, pearl earrings, with slightly wavy hair." Far from all smells of kitchen and vegetables, fragrant with imported perfume, she waits for her long-lost lover. "Our eyes met, wonder in hers. I smiled. She is wondering whether I am Asit Majumdar. Perhaps she has not seen him in a long time. Won't I do just as well for her?" It seems that she really has no choice because the hero has decided to have her as his own.

If the hero is so disposed towards his would-be lovers, his friendships are not very different either. Dipu, the young hero of the novel *Jiban Jerekam* (As Life Is), serves as a good example of the craving that Sunil's heroes display in general for self-importance. In him it is more telling because he is less vicious, less pompous, somewhat amoral in a naive way. It is also worth noting that his consciousness is the lens through which we view the world. Here again the very first pages establish the salient traits of the hero. Our first glimpse of him is at lunch in a small town. He is on vacation. The postman knocks on his door, upon which a friend, Arup, gets up to receive a telegram. Normally this would be considered a helpful gesture and left at that. But our hero does not see it this way. He loads this act with meaning and sees in it nothing except Arup's officiousness and his habitual self-regard. Arup, it becomes quickly apparent, is an object of competition for the hero, mainly because he is from a wealthy family. The competition begins at levels such as this: "During their week at Chaibasha Arup had received three letters and Dipu none. And now a telegram!" This prepares us for a sustained pattern of one-upmanship through the rest of the novel. Others may receive petty love letters, but Dipu's is a telegram, and that too about his father's heart attack! Who knows but that he may even be dead by now! At once Dipu becomes the centre of attention, the holiday mood vanishes, and Arup offers to accompany him back to Calcutta. Dipu accepts this, but not without a negative reflection about Arup's eagerness. While he enjoys the attention, he maintains a distance as well. His distance and silence are interpreted by the others as intensity, and he is admired for not seeking sympathy. His friends admire this silent, strong man. "Dipu is in a shock due to the telegram, but being a deep and introverted person, cannot express anything." Dipu himself, however, is basking in the reflected glory of his relatives in spite of his emotional crisis. He breaks the silence in order to talk about his rich and famous uncle.

> Dipu couldn't hide a touch of pride from his voice. Drawing in a full breath, he said, "My own uncle is a famous doctor in Calcutta, charges sixty-four rupees for each visit. Dr R P Sarkar. Haven't you heard of him?"

In spite of the fact that Dipu calls people like Arup his friend and runs away to Paramesh when Calcutta becomes intolerable, he credits them with little besides stupidity, pompousness, hypocrisy, or at best a crude affection. This hypercritical approach, however, does not prevent him from using their good offices. Even the tidiness of Arup becomes the object of sarcasm. "A very tidy boy, that Arup. He folds even his dirty shirts. Dipu of course can see no reason for doing this. He himself just crumples them up." But this attitude does not contradict the fact that "Dipu has planned to ask Arup to pack his suitcase as well. That should be fun." One wonders for whom or why?

If one also wonders why Dipu is so upset with Arup throughout the novel, the clue seems to lie in the following observation:

> Arup and his family are very rich *these days*. Their house is teeming with people, and once a month a doctor comes to check up on his father's health. Doctors like the uncle that Dipu boasted about are summoned to treat even headaches in their family. [Italics mine]

So Arup's family is a member of the rising bourgeoisie, the despised "nouveau riche," whereas Dipu's is a dying feudal one. The newly rich may be despised by the now-impoverished feudal families, but never ignored. Mostly they are to be resented. They have usurped a power that should have devolved to Dipu by birthright.

Young men such as Dipu are bound to be alienated and lonely. But there are some compensations. The counterpart of this world-despising loneliness is a world-engulfing megalomania - a sense of his inherent superiority in the scheme of things. Dipu, for instance, is gifted with visions, premonitions and extrasensory perception. This makes him a very unusual person indeed, since he becomes something of a poet (visions) and a prophet (premonitions). This unusual being, though he may not be rich, has always to be right. For instance, even in the hurry to reach his dying father Dipu hopes that Paramesh won't be able to find a jeep. Why? Because he has a premonition to that effect. And of course he is right, and furthermore this is seen as a victory. The prosaic and bureaucratic powers of an administrator defeated by the spiritual power of the extraordinary young man. He is reassured of his innate superiority. He does not have to *do* anything to be a hero, he just *is* one.

From the position of prophet to that of demigod is not a far cry. The hero in *Tumi Ke?* (Who Are You?) is convinced that he is constituted of the same substance as that of divinity.

> "Maya, do you recognize me?"
> "No, who are you? . . . You seem familiar, yet I don't know you."
> "Don't just concentrate on the exterior. Look within All men share something of the quality of God - can you not recognize my other self?"

Earlier too he had referred to the Advaita philosophy to reinforce his ego.

> What is that verse? Only the Brahman is real and the world is an illusion. The world - an illusion? If that is true then who can prevent me

> from *being the lord of this illusory creation?* Woman of the train, are you also an illusion? *Then you are also mine.* If Brahman alone is real, then as long as I exist I am also real, and *equally real is the fact that you are mine.* [Italics mine]

Though this version of monism would have thoroughly baffled its originator Shankaracharya, it does serve a purpose for the hero. Compounding confusion through phoniness, mysticism and garbled logic, the hero reaches a climax in his fantasy of power, which is finally directed to the acquisition of the woman as a piece of private property. It should be noted with what fervour and how often he uses the possessive pronoun *mine* in the context of a human relationship.

This need to own people and objects can be severely threatened by the existence of previous ownership or an inability to compete. Then the ability to fantasize comes to the hero's rescue, and imagination is put to profit. In *Tumi Ke?* the hero speaks of his fascination for a house that he would really like to own.

> Almost nothing could be seen of it from the outside - it was surrounded by such high walls . . . on top of which were inset pieces of glass. We had heard that the owner was a very luxurious person, and had planted all sorts of rare flowers and fruit trees there. But it was impossible to enter it - only very distinguished people could enter by asking for special permission.

It is evident that not only does he wish to own this house, but he also wants to belong to the exclusive world of the owner. Failing both, he uses binoculars to get a closer view, which leads to the following speculation:

> As a child I didn't quite see it like that, but afterwards, whenever I thought of this house, I felt that though another person may own its physical form, *even I own the beauty of it. I can say that that house was mine, because I enjoyed the beauty of it. This is how one can own everything in this world.* At the very most only binoculars are necessary. [Italics mine]

His aesthetic is one of possession, where even seeing and enjoying can become a form of owning. The language of private property is ever present in his discussion about beauty and love. It seems that he is incapable of experiencing the world except by transforming it, at least metaphorically, into private property.

The sexuality of Sunil's hero, needless to say, is closely linked with fantasies for power and domination. And this power he acquires through an actual or symbolic ownership, which reduces the women to the objective status of private property. But since the other side of this quest of power is a feeling of powerlessness, the hero presents us with a curious dynamic of aggression and insecurity. Egoism and competitiveness contain traits of infantility, which are most clearly visible in his relationship with his parents. We must consider this before we can understand the nature of his sexuality.

The hero's relationship with his father, similar to that with friends, is fraught with dependency and competitiveness. His response to the death or illness of the father figure underscores this dependency. This theme of the death or illness of the father is present in most of the ten novels that I studied. The dying father functions as a dying god, and his decay or death changes the world from order to chaos. The source of authority disappears, and morality becomes a subjective and relative matter. The hero, a lost child, wanders through the chaos, blaming the father all the while for his present condition. But that is not all. If the hero is a dependent child, he is also an aggressive one. Much as he laments the death of his father, he also seems to need it, since in his hunger for power he can tolerate no competitors. The older male must be killed for the child to own what once belonged to him. The drive to ownership and consequent competitiveness leads to oedipal patricide. In the novel *Gavira Gopana* (In the Secret Depths), the young hero Tapu pushes the limits to their farthest by indulging in all sorts of sexual liberties, with a clear awareness that any knowledge of this might kill his father. In fact, as the father dwindles into nothingness, Tapu grows into a man. The old patriarch, then, must die, for the new patriarch to assert himself, though he must go through a period of chaos and growing pains in the process.

What does the old patriarch possess that distinguishes him as such? He possesses an absolute authority over one woman in particular, or women figures in general. He is the legitimate owner of the hero's mother, and the hero is prepared to fight him on that score. Submission, endurance and self-sacrifice, the ideals of womanhood, embodied by the mother, must serve him as well. Sometimes he actualizes this incestuous sexuality by entering into relationships with mother surrogates, such as older relatives. In *Gavira Gopana* for instance, the young hero is sexually awakened by his middle-aged aunt. Or the complex and ambivalent relationship with a sister (present in most of the novels) forms a corollary to the main theme of incest. This incestuous feeling towards the sister often takes the form of a violent protectiveness. It masquerades as the old convention of defending the family honour. The hero of *Pratidwandi* (The Adversary) is more outraged than his mother when he learns that his sister is promiscuous. Dipu in *Jiban Jerekam* reacts with extraordinary prudishness and annoyance, is shocked to "the core of his being" when he learns that his obsequious and dependent sister is considering divorce in order to remarry.

However, when an actual relationship with a female relative is not present in the novels, when there is no woman whom the hero can take for granted and whose unquestioning loyalty, submission and nurturing he can rely on, he projects his needs onto the norms of womanhood. The orphan hero of *Mesh, Brishti, Alo* (Cloud, Rain and Sun) makes a statement to the effect that his wife or fiancee must fill up the gap left in his life by the death of his mother. This makes perfect sense in view of the fact that women are the only group of people with whom the hero does not compete. It is not even a possibility which he considers. He is quite convinced that women were created for the purpose of comforting and consoling men, who in their turn were created to compete with each other. There is not much that men can offer each other in the way of love or comfort. As Dipu puts it:

> Male touch is generally repulsive to me, especially more so if the male is unknown. I have never walked with my arm around a friend's shoulder . . .

It is no wonder then that this rugged and lonely individual relies on women a great deal - for support and self-worth. They tend to love and adore him unquestioningly. The virtuous woman, who doesn't sleep with men unless the vow is pronounced, and the bad one, who doesn't wait until the bargain is struck, both adore him with a slavishness. He marries the good woman and uses the other as he pleases since she is nothing more than a whore. Dipu, for example, during his train ride with Shanta, voices the hero's view on such matters. They are in an empty railway compartment. Shanta is leaning against him and he is caressing her face gently. But in the middle of all this,

> Dipu was a little puzzled by something. Shanta was sitting right next to him, the compartment totally deserted, yet there was no madness waking in him. No ravisher had started to rage in his veins. *"Shanta belongs to me"* - this very thought was tranquilizing. *There was no need to rush here.* But a few years ago at his aunt's house in Creak Row, if he ever met Shubhra by herself, how restless he would feel! He had a terrible curiosity about her body, and even at the risk of being caught,

> he would grab hold of her. . . But now Dipu realized that it was not love but greed. Today - even in this secluded spot - it wouldn't do to behave like that. *His entire joy and excitement consisted of the belief - "Shanta is mine."* [Italics mine]

Security of possession, the freedom to treat another person like private property, is the most significant aspect of his relationship with women. This gives him the kind of joy that the happy owner feels when he locks up an expensive jewel in a bank's vault - "Shanta is mine." A live, changing and sexually demanding woman is too much of a threat to his ego. She is the whore who resists permanent ownership, in contradistinction to the other. Therefore Shanta, the good woman, puts the final seal on her purity by going one step further than Dipu in nullifying the demands of the flesh. Unlike Shubhra, whose nose is a little too thick, body a little too full, lips a little too pouting, and palms a little too moist, who warms up very quickly to sexual advances, Shanta, with her aquiline nose, straight, tall figure, and a pure smile, "moves Dipu's hand and gets up. Then says, 'Isn't this nice? You sit here and I'll go over there to that corner, from there we'll talk to each other very loudly.' " Not intimacy, but possession is also her obsession - that of space. She is more interested in inhabiting each corner of the room to make it peculiarly her own than in the immediate closeness of her lover. She will never threaten Dipu's masculinity.

The marriageable woman in Sunil's novels is always virginal and something of a little girl. But she is also capable of protecting or soothing as only a mother can. She is a child and a woman combined. In *Saral Satya* (The Simple Truth), for instance, the only vivid description of the woman is as a child through the nostalgic eyes of her middle-aged and depraved lover. This child, however, can be made into a mother with perfect ease through male sexual imposition, but she never has any sexuality in or for herself. Her womanhood is entirely male defined.

If we move beyond the strictly personal relationships of the hero to that with society, we notice that it is often one of criticism and despair, since he is often aware of corruption and disintegration. Calcutta, the city, with its crowds, filth, crime and political ferment, is the main symbol of corruption and degeneration. It is Calcutta that destroys Himanshu in *Purusha* (The Man), or annihilates the innocence of Siddhartha *(Pratidwandi)* or Tapu (*Gavira Gopana*). The heroes are always aware of the death of an old moral and social order. They note that everything has been reduced to the state of commodity, and the world has become a huge marketplace. Prostitution, literally or metaphorically, as a type of conduct, is a key theme in these novels. Violence is omnipresent. Young, unemployed, sex-starved males in tight pants carrying steel knuckle-dusters roam the streets of Calcutta like hungry wolves. They destroy any semblance of stability in the Bengali middle-class society by indulging simultaneously in suicidal and homicidal activities.

The surface of lumpen life in Calcutta is often portrayed convincingly by Sunil Gangyopadhyay, and his novels are replete with a stance of moral revulsion. But interestingly enough, there is also an acceptance of corruption as inevitable, as "the way of the world." The simple transition from innocence to experience on which he builds his characters is also paired by the romantic opposition of the country and the city. Childhood must be always pastoral, the countryside a land of bliss; cities, on the contrary, are inevitably corrupt and decadent, places of experience. Nowhere does he question the real nature of rural existence, nor the fatalism implied in his view of cities as the modern jungles. In fact he adopts an altogether different tactic. He prizes the confrontation with this decadence, and the eventual hardening and cynicism of his heroes, as a sort of spirituality. In this context we must remember the popularity of Baudelaire's "Paris Spleen" during the early and mid sixties, as well as the coteries then formed around Alan Ginsberg and Peter Orlovsky. Baudelaire, it must be remembered, was translated into Bengali by several Bengali poets, the most notable translation being that of Buddhadeva Bose in the early sixties. Sometimes Sunil's portrayal of cities contains an echo of Baudelaire, but his "fleur de mal" is distinctly a pastiche, a petit bourgeois flirtation with self-destruction.

Though the hero suffers in this corrupt place, the anguish becomes questionable due to the fact that this corruption of the cities offers the hero an ego upliftment. While he adopts a posture of judgement, he also uses this as an excuse for cynical opportunism, irresponsibility and insensitivity. The daily suffering does not create any solidarity between him and others living in the same world. In none of the novels examined here does the hero associate with the people from the same impoverished background - young men who are facing the same problems of poverty, unemployment, family disintegration. For the hero, such people are to be avoided, their problems ignored or attributed to their lack of enterprise, intelligence and initiative. The "bootstrap" economic philosophy of North America is also that of our hero. It seems that success is the only measure of man.

If this is the hero's attitude towards those who, like himself, have not questioned this rat race, how does he feel about those unwilling to accept the present situation, who seek some means for social change? If he is full of contempt for his idle peer group, what does he think of those who go beyond a fatalism or personal careerism?

Sunil's portraits of the young left-wing activist are worth some attention. These activists are usually the younger male members of lower middle-class households, or come from a background of decaying country gentry. Frequently they are the younger brothers of the now experienced and disillusioned heroes. There is reason to believe that the hero, in his innocent, naive phase, had taken part in politics and tasted the futility of it all. But there is another difference between them, namely, that the hero was always highly imaginative and sensitive and compared to him the younger generation is definitely obtuse. The hero could never be so disrespectful to elders, so immune to family feelings, or so impervious to the question of a sister's honour, as are the younger men. And when Sunil can neither ignore nor detract from the merits of an individual's action, he introduces purely personal motives, which help to subvert its nature as political action.

Finally comes the task of assessing the author's own attitude to the ethic of his heroes. My statements have hitherto depended on the characters and their relationships. But now I must draw attention to the fact that Sunil Gangyopadhyay has no problem of contradiction with his heroes. The fact that he portrays their sufferings and loneliness as credible and legitimate without placing them within a critical perspective testifies to that. In these novels he provides no sort of alternative value framework - all is seen as sifted through the consciousness of the protagonists. There is no attempt at irony, not even where the hero's sense of himself has reached ludicrously grandiose proportions. There is no attempt to create any distance between the reader and the character through the intervention of a critical authorial voice. In fact what is encouraged through the technique of a type of naturalism is a total identification of the reader with the character. We are asked to feel, not to think. And it seems that had the author chosen to, he could have fallen back on even conventional narrative devices to accomplish a critical perception. A very common device could have been to introject a sporadic authorial aside, which speaks to the reader, behind the hero's back as it were. He could have set up a critical framework for the novel as a whole. He might have used the convention of endowing other characters with a degree of credibility equal to that of the hero and permitting them to introduce a degree of criticism or negativity into the dominant mode. But no characters are ever developed to such an extent, nor do they indulge in critical reflections about either the hero or the world in which they all live. The technique of interior monologue is used instead and awarded to the hero, which, adding a touch of psychology, offers an inside view. This serves the further function of promoting identification between the hero and the readers, creating the illusion of his being a "real person" like "us." This does not promote a critical distance, especially since we often tend to follow the dictum that "to understand is to forgive." There is also the fact that no other character is sensitive, intelligent, and passionate as the hero. The others are basically foils for the purpose of bringing out the hero's greatness. So where no attempt has been made to separate out the hero from the author, it is not unreasonable to conclude that he is the voice of the author and enjoys his approval. The device of the first-person narrative, used frequently, tends to fuse this distinction very successfully, and draws the reader even closer to the hero. It is also to be noted that where there is an unknown, third-person narrator, he prefaces sentences often with "and then he thought . . ." thereby providing almost a first-person insight.

Added to all of the above there is also tonality. Where the hero is concerned, the author always maintains a serious and protective tone. At no point does he encourage laughter about even the most trivial aspects of the hero's life. From all of this I can not but come to the conclusion that we are meant to accept this alienated, anguished being in all seriousness, at face value, on his own terms. In this also I see an advocacy - an advocacy for an ethic, which might be termed a capitalist ethic. This advocacy is carried out not only through the didacticism of the hero's socio-moral reflections, but also through a form of personal deduction by using, as I mentioned above, techniques of the psychological novel. An appeal is made to our own sense of egoism, privation and loss of control. We are titillated in our individualism and possessiveness, and we are discouraged from being critical. This appeal is enhanced by the fact that not only are the heroes ruthless competitors, seekers after wealth, but also men with visions and poetry as well. Whichever way the dice fall, they always win. With such an access to the best of both worlds, who would not want to be a lonely hero? Who would not buy alienation to get out of the fate of being a member of a faceless crowd?

Sources

The chapters in this book have appeared previously in various forms in the following publications.

"Nostalgia for the Future: The Poetry of Ernesto Cardenal" in *Fuse* (Summer: 17-28) 1984.

"The Poetry of Dionne Brand" in D Dance (ed.), *Fifty Caribbean Writers: A Bio-bibliographic Critical Sourcebook,* New York: Greenwood Press 1986.

"Andrei Tarkovsky: A Discourse on Desire and History" in *Point Counterpoint* (Vol 2 No 10: 57-61) 1986.

"Evenings Out: Political Theatre in West Bengal" in *Borderlines* (Vol 14: 25-31) 1989.

"Language and Liberation: A Study of Political Theatre in West Bengal" in *Ariel* (October: 137-144) 1984.

"Representation and Class Politics in the Theatre of Utpal Dutt"; "Nation and Class in Communist Aesthetic and the Theatre of Utpal Dutt." Occasional Paper No 106, Centre for Studies in Social Sciences, Calcutta, 1988.

"One Woman, Two Women, Without Women: Gender Construction in Bengali Theatre" in *Fuse* (Fall: 23-28) 1985.

"The Alienated Hero in the Novels of Sunil Gangyopadhyay" in *The Toronto South Asian Review* (Vol 1 No 3: 45-56) 1983.

All the Bengali texts quoted in this book were translated by the author.

Himani Bannerji was born in 1942 in Bangladesh, which was then part of preindependence India. Educated in Calcutta and Toronto she now teaches social science at York University. Her poetry, short stories, critical articles and film and theatre reviews have appeared in numerous magazines. She has published two collections of poetry, *A Separate Sky* (1982), and *doing time* (1986).